How to Give to Charity

Jessica Williams

howtogivetocharity.org

ICON BOOKS

Published in the UK in 2006
by Icon Books Ltd., The Old Dairy,
Brook Road, Thriplow, Cambridge SG8 7RG
email: info@iconbooks.co.uk
www.iconbooks.co.uk

Sold in the UK, Europe, South Africa
and Asia by Faber and Faber Ltd.,
3 Queen Square, London WC1N 3AU
or their agents

Distributed in the UK, Europe, South Africa
and Asia by TBS Ltd., Frating Distribution Centre,
Colchester Road, Frating Green, Colchester CO7 7DW

Published in Australia in 2006
by Allen & Unwin Pty. Ltd.,
PO Box 8500, 83 Alexander Street,
Crows Nest, NSW 2065

Distributed in Canada by Penguin Books Canada,
90 Eglinton Avenue East, Suite 700,
Toronto, Ontario M4P 2YE

ISBN 1 84046 699 5

Text copyright © 2006 Jessica Williams

The author has asserted her moral rights.

No part of this book may be reproduced in any form, or by any means,
without prior permission in writing from the publisher.

Typesetting by Wayzgoose

Printed and bound in the UK by Bookmarque Ltd.

Acknowledgements

Thanks to everyone who we spoke to about the issues in the book, on and off the record – you helped to form a picture of a vibrant, complex and passionate sector. Extra-special thanks go to Wendy Green and Catherine Walker at the Charities Aid Foundation, who were so enthusiastic about this project and so generous with their time and resources.

To Andrew Furlow, Ruth Tidball, Helen Sampson and all the crew at Icon Books and Faber – you guys are fantastic. Thank you for absolutely everything you've done. And to Nicholas Waddell, huge thanks for being such a good researcher – your expertise, contacts and patience were beyond helpful.

And finally, a big and heartfelt thank you to my friend Sola, for understanding the restorative powers of a glass of wine; to my boss Jez, who hates being called my boss, but was fantastically supportive throughout; to my family, whose love and support means the world, despite being half a world away; to my friends and colleagues for their love and inspiration; and to John, for everything, always.

Author's Note

As well as talking about how to give to charity, this book has charitable aspirations of its own. I've pledged all the royalty payments I'd otherwise receive to charity, and Icon Books have very generously agreed to match my contributions with donations of their own.

We'd also like to know where you would like us to spend the money. The book's website (www.howtogivetocharity.org) will have a page where you can vote for your favourite charity – or alternatively you can write in with your own suggestions. After all, one of the aims of this book is to get everybody thinking and talking about charity, so we'd love to hear from you.

About the Author

Jessica Williams is the author of the bestselling *50 Facts that Should Change the World*. 'A research handbook for the *No Logo* generation' (*Guardian*), it was described as 'fearless and compelling' by Monica Ali. Jessica is a BBC journalist and producer of the News 24 discussion programme *Hardtalk*.

Contents

	Introduction	1
1	The World of Charity	7
2	Charity and the Law	31
3	Why Should I Give to Charity?	47
4	Why Do People Say I Shouldn't Give to Charity?	53
5	OK, So I Want to Give – How?	85
6	Resources	109
	Notes	151
	Index	160

Introduction

On 26 December 2004, a huge earthquake shook the sea floor under the Indian Ocean. Some measurements put it at 9.3 on the Richter scale, making it the second-largest earthquake ever recorded on a seismograph. The massive movement of the seabed displaced an enormous volume of water and the resulting tsunami devastated coastal areas of Indonesia, Sri Lanka, South India and Thailand. As Britain woke up after another heavy Christmas of eating and drinking, the pictures on television screens of death and destruction were shocking.

At the time of writing, the death toll stood at around 273,000. It's likely a final figure will never be reached, as many bodies were swept out to sea and will never be recovered. Around the world, people watched horrified at the unfolding tragedy. People scanned newspapers and websites, sent texts and e-mails trying to find out if people they knew in the region were safe. In the rich Western world, we heard about the rapidly mobilising relief effort, about the urgent need for funds to help provide food and medical care and to begin to bury the dead. And we gave.

It's not an exaggeration to say that people gave more to help the victims of the tsunami than they ever had. Eighty-one per cent of Britain's adult population gave money. Even after the huge consumer frenzy of Christmas, the average adult gave £41 to the appeal – contrast this with the £12 that the average Briton gives to charity each month. Over two-thirds of Britons said they'd given more to this appeal than they ever had.[1]

Groups organising appeals for tsunami relief were amazed at the generosity of ordinary people. In Britain, the Disasters Emergency Committee raised £350 million in two months.[2] A remarkable £250 million of this came from individuals. And just two weeks after the tsunami hit, Médecins Sans Frontières (MSF) announced that the appeal had been so successful that it would no longer accept donations to the tsunami fund, as it had all the money that it needed for its work in the region.[3]

MSF's decision was widely criticised by the charity sector, and the French government immediately issued a plea for its citizens to keep giving to other charities. But it also brought into sharp focus the effect of the 24-hour media coverage of the tsunami disaster. MSF pointed out that it had taken just eight days to raise 40 million euros for the tsunami – while it took two months to raise 650,000 euros for the victims of civil war in Darfur, Sudan.

The tsunami was a huge story for the Western media. There were thousands of Europeans and Americans missing. The period between Christmas and New Year is traditionally quiet in the news media, providing all the more air-time and column inches for pictures and stories of the devastation. Charities acknowledged the clear link between heavy media coverage and public donations, and more than two-thirds of Britons mentioned that the harrowing images in the media had driven them to give.[4]

Behind the headlines, though, lurked another story. What impact would this generosity have on charitable giving as a whole – and would other charities suffer? Sixteen per cent of Britons who gave to the tsunami appeal said they would not have much more to give to charities in 2005.[5] Indeed, a number of charities reported that they had experienced a drop in income since the tsunami appeal. The World Food Programme told *The Times* that donations to its African operations had dropped by 21 per cent in January 2005 compared with the year before. The Royal National Lifeboat Institution and Macmillan Cancer Relief both said they had experienced a fall in income.[6]

But there were heartening signs, too. The tsunami appeals offered new ways for people to give – via text message, the internet or telephone. Half of the larger gifts were made tax-efficiently (we'll talk about what this means in Chapter 5), meaning the charities received even more money. More than 10 per cent of people who gave to the tsunami said they'd give more to charity in future – and these people tended to be younger donors.[7]

So will this be, as the Sri Lankan ambassador to the US put it, 'a transforming event'[8] – or will it come to be seen as a one-off act of generosity by people in rich countries?

The charity sector in Britain is taking a close look at itself, wondering what can be done to turn casual givers (like those who gave to the tsunami appeal) into lifetime supporters. The government has announced wide-ranging reform of the laws which govern charities in Britain – not before time, as the current legal framework dates back 400 years and really isn't in touch with what modern society considers to be charity. And two big non-profit umbrella groups – the National Council for Voluntary Organisations and the Association of Chief Executives of Voluntary Organisations – have launched a consultation into how the sector should look in ten years.

For people working in the sector, then, there will be huge changes. But what will this mean for the rest of us? For one thing, competition between charities will become even more intense and the average donor will see more and greater demands on them to give money, time and resources to charities. The British government has already undertaken a raft of initiatives aimed at encouraging citizens to give money and volunteer, and the sector would like to see it doing even more. Simply put, deciding how and where we'd like to give is going to become a very important question.

To be honest, most people probably don't spend a great deal of time thinking about why and how to give to charity. We give because someone's asked us for money or because a particular cause inspires us – not because we sit down one day and think 'I've got a bit of spare cash, who could I give it to?' That's probably why two-thirds of British people surveyed said that if they had an extra £20 a week to spend, they wouldn't give it to charity – but more than half said that if their favourite charity was in need, they'd happily give more.[9] But in the wake of the tsunami in South-East Asia in 2004, many people gave to charity who'd never given before. Chances are, if you gave to the tsunami, you saw the difference your money could make. And you'd like to do it again. That's where this book can help.

This book will tell you everything you need to know about how charities work and what they do. We'll look at the laws governing charities, how they're changing and how that will affect people who support them. We'll examine why you should give to charity at all – and check out some of the arguments you often hear against giving to charity. And then we'll look at how to make sure your money is working as hard as it can for your chosen charity, as well as looking at a few of the more unusual ways in which you can give your time and money. Finally, we've compiled a resources section which will give you lists of places to go to find out more and provide you with a few starting points to work out your own best giving strategy.

1

The World of Charity

Charity is full of contrasts and contradictions. The oldest charities in the UK have been operating continuously since the 5th or 6th century AD. The largest ones operate multi-million-pound budgets, employ thousands of staff and are working at the cutting edge of scientific research and international policy. The smallest are working to save village halls and church steeples: they're staffed completely by volunteers and might have an annual income of just a few hundred pounds.

So given that degree of diversity, it's remarkable that the UK's charity law is still largely influenced by an Elizabethan statute that's more than 400 years old. The 1601 law spoke about 'Maintenance of sicke and maymed Souldiers and Marriners', about support 'for Mariages of poore Maides' and 'younge tradesmen Handicraftesmen and persons decayed'. For hundreds of years these laws have been adapted, stretched and made to fit a world where the roles of charity may have changed, but the legal system has not.

It's no wonder then that some of us feel a bit confused.

Nearly 90 per cent of British people don't know that Eton College (where pupils pay annual boarding fees of some £20,000) is a registered charity. More than a quarter believe that the Child Support Agency is a charity – it's actually a government agency.[10]

We understand that charities play a huge role in society; but sometimes, it seems, we don't quite know what that role is. Every so often there are stories in the media which decry the 'fat-cat' salaries paid to charity staff. True, some salaries to the CEOs of the biggest charities are generous, but then consider the work they do: Sir Paul Nurse, the head of Cancer Research UK, may be paid £140,000 a year, but he is a Nobel-Prize-winning scientist with a huge amount of expertise in his field and his job involves administering an income of £305 million, thousands of staff and tens of thousands of supporters. It seems we still expect charity workers to have large private incomes and work for nothing. We also don't like charities to have close links with government or business.

But despite these concerns, British people have a great loyalty to charity. Almost all of us give every year in some way. We feel passionately about charity and philanthropy in a way that we never could about the private sector. And this enthusiasm for giving time and money to help others has a long history. In fact, some people even suggest that philanthropy is an essential part of the human condition.

A very short history of giving

It might seem outrageous that Britain's charity laws have remained the same for four centuries – but those laws are relative youngsters when brought into the historical context of charity. The idea of doing good works for those less fortunate than oneself is a human tradition that dates back to the earliest civilisations. As far back as 2300 BC, an Egyptian ruler called Harkhuf insisted on being buried with a record of his charitable acts inscribed on the wall of his tomb: 'I gave bread to the hungry, clothing to the naked, I ferried him who had no boat.' In 600 BC a fund was established to help the children of soldiers killed in the war in Attica.[11] The Li Ki, the Chinese 'Book of Rites' that documents religious practices between 800 and 500 BC, details special attention that was given to needy people in society. Religions also explicitly set out charity as an important part of the practice of faith. It's a translation of the Greek word *agape*, which means divine, unconditional, self-sacrificing love. Christian theology holds charity to be the greatest of the three virtues (the others being faith and hope). The concept of zakat is one of the five pillars of Islam and requires all able-bodied Muslims to give alms to needy people. The word means both 'purification' and 'growth'.

Judaism posits tzedakah as a crucial tradition. The scholar Maimonides (1135–1204) set out the different levels of tzedakah, the lowest of which was giving unwillingly, the highest giving a poor person work or lending him money to start a business and thus freeing him from the need to rely on charity.

Obviously poor and needy people benefited from this generosity – but the motives for giving weren't completely altruistic. By the time that Geoffrey Chaucer was writing his *Canterbury Tales* in mediaeval England, helping the poor was thought to help reduce the amount of time that one's soul would spend in purgatory. Indeed, in Chaucer's time the poor served a very important purpose, providing wealthy people with the opportunity to do good deeds and increase their social standing. Gifts weren't well organised and many of the donations had a lot more to do with the wishes of the donors than the needs of the poor.

The late 15th and early 16th centuries saw huge social change in Britain. The feudal system of land ownership and tenure was breaking down, and many people lost the land that their families had worked for generations. Towns grew in size and many destitute people were forced to turn to crime.[12] Tudor governments realised that private donations would play an important part in helping to supplement the statutory system of poor relief.[13] In order to best regulate this, the Statute of Charitable Uses was enacted in 1601 – incredibly, it's still the foundation of much of the UK's charity regulation.

Around the time of the Industrial Revolution, charity was no longer an indulgence of the very rich – it was becoming a moral obligation of anyone who was not in need of help themselves. Isabella Beeton, famous for her

The five oldest charities in the UK

According to a survey carried out by the Charity Commission in 2001,[14] the UK's five oldest charities have all been going for more than 1,000 years. Four out of the five are schools.

Charity	Year established
The King's School, Canterbury	597
Rochester Cathedral Grammar School	604
St Peter's School, York	627
Thetford Grammar School, Norfolk	631
St John's Winchester Hospital	935

cookbooks, set out in her *Book of Household Management* (1861) that the new middle-class housewife was expected to use her own domestic skills to help the poor. 'There is scarcely any income so small but something may be spared from it,' she wrote, 'even if it be but "the widow's mite".'[15]

Charity was certainly widespread in Victorian society – it's hard to put an exact figure on the amount that was distributed, but by the late 1800s there were some 700 charities in London alone. It was said that in the 1880s the income of London's charities was greater than that of several states combined:

London spends the revenue of many a Continental State on the unfortunate within her gates. Her wisdom in the distribution of her abundant alms is very much disputed; but her liberality is, beyond compare, the most copious of any known community. No single fact more forcibly illustrates the enormous trade of London, than the million sterling which the metropolitan pocket disgorges at the call of charity.[16]

Certain employers attempted to take care of their workers through philanthropy: George Cadbury created a model village near Birmingham for the workers at his cocoa and chocolate factory while the industrialist Robert Owen, disgusted by the conditions in the woollen mills of Edinburgh and Glasgow, set up schools and welfare programmes at his New Lanark mills.

There were also philanthropists who gave large endowments to the arts and learning: Henry Tate made his fortune in the sugar-refining business and donated his art collection to what would become the Tate galleries, while the Scottish-American businessman Andrew Carnegie gave a large part of his vast personal wealth to establish libraries, schools and universities (among many other projects). In his essay 'The Gospel of Wealth' Carnegie set out his thoughts on the responsibilities which came with wealth:

There is but one right mode of using enormous fortunes – namely, that the possessors from time to time during their own lives should so administer these as to promote the permanent good to the communities from which they were gathered ... public sentiment would soon say of one who died possessed of available wealth which he was free to administer: 'The man who dies thus rich dies disgraced.'[17]

More than a hundred years later, many super-rich businesspeople are following the example of the Victorian philanthropists by setting up their own private foundations. And the rest of us – who haven't yet amassed our 'enormous fortunes' – are carrying on Victorian traditions too, by giving what we can when we can.

How does the sector look now?

Today almost everyone gives each year. Research by the Charities Aid Foundation and the National Council for Voluntary Organisations showed that in a typical month in 2003, just under two-thirds of Britons gave. Most of them gave through traditional, small-change methods – street collections, buying raffle tickets, buying something in a charity shop. At the other end of the scale, there are the elite givers: fewer than one in twenty people give more than £50 a month, but they generate well over half of the total amount donated.

Although the tsunami appeal inspired many headlines about the new-found generosity of the British public, there had long been a suggestion that things might be getting better for the non-profit sector. The *Economist* magazine mused in July 2004 that there might be a 'new golden age of philanthropy', although they were talking less about dropping 50p in a collection box, and more about establishing multi-million-dollar foundations. Once, the super-rich might have left huge bequests in their wills – now it seems they are giving more and more of it away while they are still alive. On the back of the dot.com boom, there has been an explosion of private philanthropic foundations in America – and there are signs that something similar is happening in Europe.[18]

According to Paul Schervish, a US-based academic who has done substantial research into philanthropy, 'For the first time in history, more and more people have more money than they want to leave to their kids.'[19] Look at Bill Gates, whose Bill & Melinda Gates Foundation is now endowed with approximately $28 billion.

But although there might be more money around for charities, there is also a lot more competition. There are currently 167,000 charities in England and Wales, with 200,000 more community and neighbourhood groups. Six thousand new charities are formed each year.[20] And while big charities may be flourishing, there are many smaller bodies that are struggling to raise funds.

So which are the charitable sectors that attract the big donations? Do we give to the same causes that our grandparents did? And which are the mega-charities that attract hundreds of millions of pounds of donations each year?

What are the most popular charitable causes?

There's an old cliché that British people care more about animals than they do about people – but patterns of charitable giving in the UK put people pretty high up the list. Animal charities are always popular, but so are cancer charities. And analysis of the sector over the past 25 years shows that increasingly British donors are changing their priorities.

For instance, events like Live Aid and the increasing reach of television have made Western donors far more aware of the various problems faced in poor countries. Even before the tsunami donations were taken into account, international aid was the most popular sector for charity giving in 2004.

In addition to this, the kind of donations we are making to health charities is changing. The Charities Aid Foundation notes:

> As people have become more aware of health issues they have changed their support, with charities for chest and heart problems becoming more popular. 25 years ago we were just becoming aware of the risks of HIV and AIDS and no major charities helped in this area ... Charities for those with physical disabilities and the blind seem to have become less popular with donors over the last 25 years although this could be because they have been so successful! People with disabilities are now seen more as empowered and less as victims.[21]

Charities Aid Foundation 2003-4 top ten causes by voluntary donations

	Cause	Number of charities in CAF top 500	Total voluntary income (£ millions)
1	International	31	625
2	Cancer	24	580
3	General religious causes	41	368
4	Heritage and the environment	32	363
5	Arts and culture	53	361
6	Children	33	359
7	Religious missionary causes	43	308
8	Animal protection	17	271
9	General social welfare	15	243
10	Disability	20	178

(Source: Charities Aid Foundation, cafonline.org)

How much money is given overall?

The Charity Commission calculates that the income for all the registered charities in England and Wales was nearly £35 billion in 2004. By the end of that year there were

166,000 registered charities in England and Wales, another 17,000 in Scotland and an estimated 4,000 in Northern Ireland.

The vast majority of the registered charities are very small – but the sector is dominated by large charities. Nearly 90 per cent of the money raised by the sector goes to just 7 per cent of the charities. Even among the biggest charities, the heavyweights still do the best: out of all the income raised by the top 500 charities, a quarter went to the top 10.

It's also interesting to note that while our priorities might be changing, the list of the five biggest charities has remained remarkably steady over recent years (see box overleaf).

So who gives – and who doesn't?

Individual donors play a huge part in funding Britain's charities. So-called 'voluntary income' amounts to more than half the funding received by the top 500 charities (see box on page 19).

It's thought that in Britain almost all of us give to charity in the course of a year. This can include any number of different things – dropping a few coins in a collection bucket, volunteering to coach a local kids' sports team, buying a lottery ticket – but almost everyone supports charity in some way. In a typical month, 65.8 per cent of adults will give to charity, with an average donation of £12.32.[22]

Overall, women give more often than men and give more: 70.7 per cent of women give, compared with 60.1 per cent of men, and they give an average of £13.55 a month (compared

The top five ranking charities in the UK

	1986–7	1996–7	2001–2	2003–4
1	RNLI	Oxfam	Cancer Research UK	Cancer Research UK
2	The National Trust	The National Trust	Oxfam	The National Trust
3	Oxfam	Imperial Cancer Research	The National Trust	Oxfam
4	Imperial Cancer Research	Cancer Research Campaign	RNLI	British Heart Foundation
5	Cancer Research Campaign	British Heart Foundation	British Heart Foundation	RNLI

Source: Charities Aid Foundation. Note – Cancer Research Campaign and Imperial Cancer merged to form Cancer Research UK in 2002.

Sources of income to the 2003–4 CAF top 500 charities (£ millions)

Fundraising income	3,229
Legacy income	1,065
Income from the Lottery	252
Income from goods donated to shops	383
Total voluntary income	**4,930**
Government grants	1,405
Other grants	507
Other income	2,250
Total non-voluntary income	**4,163**
Total income	**9,093**

Source: Charities Aid Foundation website, cafonline.org

with £10.81 for men). And older people give more than the young: nearly three-quarters of those between 55 and 64 give an average of £16.60 per month, while a little over half of those between 16 and 24 give a monthly average of £6.56.[23] The analysts note that the age differential may be due to the differing levels in income, with young people generally having less to give away – but it doesn't explain why men, who earn more on average than women, give less.

As you might expect, poorer people give less than richer people. Research by the Charities Aid Foundation and the

NCVO has found that social classes A and B (where A is upper-middle class, higher managerial and B is middle class, intermediate managerial) give on average £28.63 to charity per month, and 76.4 per cent give every month. Contrast this with the C2 group (skilled working class), where two-thirds give each month with an average of £7.56 per month – and the D and E classes (working class and 'lowest level of subsistence') where 57.6 per cent give each month, an average of £6.11.[24]

But it's worth noting that as a *proportion* of their income, poorer households actually give more to charity. The poorest 10 per cent, who give an average of just over £2 a week, are actually giving 3 per cent of their income to charity – compared with the richest 10 per cent, who give only 1 per cent.[25]

There are three broad types of givers in the UK: the very wealthy or 'elite' givers, who give large amounts and tend to have ongoing relationships with charities; the 'faithful' givers, who give less but still do so regularly and feel involved with their particular cause; and the vast majority of people who give small amounts to people rattling buckets or buy the occasional knick-knack from a charity shop.

Charities have become adept at targeting different kinds of givers, picking out their various motivations and appealing to them:

> Lower socio-economic groups tend to see needy people as a group to be pitied because of their treatment at the hand

of fate. Promotional messages stressing the ability of even a small gift to alleviate pain and suffering are therefore likely to be most effective. The higher socio-economic groups, by contrast, particularly those from the professions, give not only for the amelioration of suffering but also for the longer-term change in their situation. Support is thus prompted by a need to make a change in a social structure, and promotional messages could perhaps reflect this motivation.[26]

For those who don't give, what's behind their decision? When asked, 23 per cent of non-givers said they couldn't afford it, 22 per cent said that charities ask for inappropriate sums, and 19 per cent said that governments should fund the work that charities do. Just 2.8 per cent said they felt charities were not deserving.[27]

Of course, some people will never give to charity no matter how many times they are asked. But charities have had some success with lowering their suggested donations (asking for small amounts like £2 a month) and making it clear that 'every penny helps', thus legitimising small gifts. There are also signs that people who wouldn't normally give can be reached — 86 per cent of people aged 18–24 donated to the tsunami appeal,[28] well above their usual levels. Thirty-seven per cent of those who gave said they weren't regular donors to charity.[29] It's thought that new methods of donating — on the internet and via text message — may help attract more young people.

What role does the government play?

As we saw earlier, the British government is very keen to encourage citizens to give to charity and to volunteer their time to good causes. It's thought that by doing this, we become involved in our communities and help to strengthen the bonds of society. The government has granted tax breaks for some forms of giving and has set up schemes to promote payroll giving and volunteering. We'll look more closely at the details of these in Chapter 5.

But as well as encouraging its citizens to give, the British government makes substantial payments to charity itself. In 2002, the first ever estimate of the total amount of government funding came to £5.06 billion – that's about a third of the total income of general household charities.[30] What's more, it's increasing year on year and is one of the main reasons that funding to charities is growing.

On the face of it, this has to be a good thing. Politicians are coming to realise that the non-profit sector plays a key role in strengthening civil society. The government is trying to foster a sense of community by encouraging people to give, and it's giving more itself. But it's also interesting to look at the relationship between those two trends.

Living in a comparatively wealthy country, we expect the government to pay for basic services, and this includes social welfare. Research by the Charities Aid Foundation has shown that people don't give as much to charities which receive large amounts of government funding because they think this means they don't have to contribute themselves. This is particularly evident with causes where people think the government should give more, like cancer, blindness, mental health and education. If a charity receives a large amount of government funding one year, individual donations will fall in the next year – so government funding may even be counter-productive to some charities.[31]

It's also worth noting that there are sectors which we think are funded by government, but which actually aren't. For example, Britain's lifeboats are funded not by the government but by the Royal National Lifeboat Institution – which is almost entirely reliant on volunteer donations.

Increased government funding has also caused a debate about the independence of the voluntary sector. International development charities which receive a large proportion of their funding from government are at particular risk of entering into a political minefield. As Arundhati Roy, writing in *Le Monde Diplomatique*, put it: 'It turns confrontation into negotiation. It depoliticises resistance. It interferes with local peoples' movements that have traditionally been self-reliant.'[32]

There is a real issue here, and it's one that is worth raising with the charities you give to. If they accept government funding, how do they seek to maintain their independence? You could ask for the charity to provide examples of how it has criticised government policy. In some cases, biting the hand that feeds isn't just wise, it's healthy.

And what about big businesses? Are they giving enough?

In a word, no. In 2001 the head of the National Council for Voluntary Organisations, Stuart Etherington, called for businesses to aim to give 1 per cent of their profits to charity. But three years on, the *Guardian*'s annual survey of corporate giving found that only 34 of the FTSE 100 companies are reaching this target. The public believes that charities get 24 per cent of their funding from big business – in reality, that figure was just 4.3 per cent in 2004, down from 4.8 per cent the year before.[33]

It's also interesting to consider the impact that the generosity towards the tsunami relief effort had on corporate giving. As it was feared, some charities reported a decrease in income – and corporate donations fell further than any other source of funding, with 36.8 per cent of charities reporting a decrease in income from companies (compared with 32.4 per cent which said individual donations had fallen).[34]

In a business climate where corporate social responsibility is much discussed, what does this seeming lack of generosity mean? The NCVO believes that companies may be looking at broader ways of helping the voluntary sector – employees may now be encouraged to volunteer, the company may take on more pro bono work or donate goods or services rather than straight cash. Businesses are also increasingly setting up separate foundations to achieve their charitable aims. There are more than 100 such foundations in the UK and these account for 11 per cent of corporate giving. And there is an increasing prominence given to cause-related marketing – where big-name brands support charitable causes in return for some warm fuzzy advertising.[35]

The government is encouraging businesses to get involved through providing tax incentives for gifts of money, property or time, and through supporting organisations like Business in the Community (BITC) and the Giving Campaign. BITC awards businesses meeting the 1 per cent giving target a PerCent Standard and gives a Community-Mark to small and medium-sized businesses which contribute to their local community.

How does Britain compare to other countries?

In 2003 British people gave £7.1 billion to charity[36] – that's around £148 per adult, but it's just 0.62 per cent of the country's gross domestic product (GDP). On the face of it, that doesn't look good. But to put it in perspective, a study of 36 countries around the world showed that just two countries give more than 1 per cent of GDP: the US and Israel.[37]

Compared with other rich countries, Americans are extremely generous. Nearly 90 per cent of households give to charity and the average annual contribution is $1,620, or £921.[38] This contrasts pretty sharply with the annual average UK donation of just under £150.[39]

Why such a huge difference? First of all, the state social welfare system in the US is far less generous than in the UK, and the American public pays less in tax – but that means American charities shoulder a lot more of the social welfare burden. In contrast, the British public pays more tax, and we feel the government should be responsible for certain things. So, as we've already discussed, Britons have often been concerned that giving to charity means the government will spend less on those causes.

The US also provides a spectacular system of tax incentives for donors to charity. One provision allows people to donate gifts in kind, like clothes or computers, and deduct the estimated value from their tax bill, while another allows donors to commit an item to charity irrevocably, like a house, a piece of art or a sum of money. The donor gets immediate tax relief but they retain some financial benefit – often interest payments – until they die, when the charity gets the gift.[40]

Americans are also far more likely to give in a planned fashion – say, via payroll giving – whereas British donors are far more likely to give when asked. Nearly 60 per cent of UK charitable donations in 2003 were spontaneous. And it's also interesting to note that British people constantly underestimate their wealth and therefore don't think they are able to make generous gifts to charity. Only 3.5 per cent of Britons describe themselves as being in the top quarter of the country by income, and nearly half say they are in the bottom quarter.[41]

Things look a little brighter when volunteering is added into the picture. When time is given a monetary value – that of the average wage of a community worker – the study calculated that some 60 per cent of private giving is in the form of volunteering. When that is taken into account alongside giving, the UK's contribution is 2.57 per cent of GDP. The US comes in close behind with 2.47 per cent. The most generous three countries are the Netherlands (4.49 per cent), Sweden (4.41 per cent) and Tanzania (3.76 per cent), and the least generous rich countries are Italy (0.8 per cent) and Japan (0.64 per cent).[42]

Four of the top five most generous countries – the Netherlands, Sweden, Norway and France – are in Western Europe. They don't fare so well when volunteering is taken out of the equation: all give an average of less than 0.4 per cent of GDP. That's likely because all four countries have high tax rates and generous social welfare systems. But their high volunteering rates come from a rich history of social movements which gave rise to strong advocacy and professional organisations. In the Nordic countries especially, voluntary activity is a key part of sports and recreational life.[43]

As for Tanzania, gifts of money make up 0.6 per cent of GDP, but when gifts of time are taken into account, it's one of the most generous countries in the world. Despite its being a poorer country than the others in the top five, it is thought that Tanzania (and Africa as a whole) has strong civil society traditions based in the informal ties along tribal and village lines.[44]

Even with our huge army of volunteers, Britons are clearly falling behind – and this is all the more concerning given that Victorian Britain arguably invented modern philanthropy. Clearly, we should give more.

Well, how much should we give, then?

The Giving Campaign – an organisation set up by the British government and the voluntary sector – suggested that every Briton should give 1 per cent of their annual income to charity. This would almost double the current average, and it would give the sector an extra £11 billion a year. To put this in perspective, this is roughly the amount needed each year to provide clean drinking water and sanitation to everyone in the world; or to reduce infant mortality, improve maternal health and combat HIV/Aids, tuberculosis and malaria by 2015 (as mandated by the UN Millennium Development Goals).[45]

That would be a good start, then – but other measures suggest a more sizeable contribution. The Church of England recommends a 'tithe' of 5 per cent of your income. The Muslim concept of zakat is interpreted to require a 2.5 per cent payment to charity on savings and valuables, and the Jewish tzedakah suggests between 10 and 20 per cent depending on a worshipper's circumstances.

People working in the not-for-profit sector are more reluctant to set benchmark figures for giving. It all depends on your personal circumstances – how much you earn, how much you can afford (not just as a one-off, but on a regular basis) and whether there are other ways you can give time, money or other gifts to charity. We'll look at some of the more inventive ways of giving in Chapter 5.

2
Charity and the Law

As we have seen, the voluntary sector handles billions of pounds of income every year and performs some extremely important functions in our society. So it's clear that some regulation is necessary – to make sure that people's generosity isn't exploited and that the money goes where it's meant to. But with modern society placing ever greater demands on charities, Britain's regulatory system is coming under more and more stress. By the time this book is published, there should be new laws in place which will reflect the modern voluntary sector. What effects might those new laws have on average donors? Read on and find out.

What is a charity?

A charity is a particular type of voluntary organisation. It will be set up to fulfil a particular aim that is defined by law as being charitable. Generally, when we say 'charity' in this book, we mean registered charities – which means the organisation has been recognised as a charity by the Charity Commission (in England and Wales) or the Office of the

Scottish Charity Regulator. (Charities in Northern Ireland cannot register – all they can do is apply to the Inland Revenue for charitable status for tax purposes.)[46]

An organisation that has charitable aims and satisfies the Commission's requirements can choose to become a registered charity. Although registered charities can take a number of different forms – some are set up as companies limited by guarantee, others as trusts or unincorporated associations – they are all independent of government or other statutory bodies, and they are not profit-making, as any surplus will be used to further the charity's aims.

The law that governs charities in Britain is largely unchanged from its original form – as enacted in the Statute of Charitable Uses of 1601, over 400 years ago. That piece of legislation is not in force any more, yet it's still remarkably influential. It's fascinating to read the original wording of the statute. The Preamble sets out the kinds of things that Elizabethans were giving money to:

> some for Releife of aged impotent and poore people, some for Maintenance of sicke and maymed Souldiers and Marriners, Schooles of Learninge, Free Schooles and Schollers in Universities, some for Repaire of Bridges Portes Havens Causwaies Churches Seabankes and Highwaies, some for Educacion and prefermente of Orphans, some for or towardes Reliefe Stocke or Maintenance of Howses of Correccion, some for Mariages of poore Maides, some for Supportacion Ayde and Helpe of younge tradesmen Handicraftesmen and persons decayed, and others for

reliefe or redemption of Prisoners or Captives, and for aide or ease of any poore Inhabitantes concerninge paymente of Fifteenes, setting out of Souldiers and other Taxes.[47]

Although this act was repealed in the 20th century, its statements of charitable purposes are still fundamental to charity law. The courts and the Charity Commission have made many decisions over the years about what constitute 'charitable purposes' and this has created a complex set of rules.

In 1891, a court case snappily titled *Income Tax Special Purpose Commissioners* v. *Pemsel* set out a classification of charitable purposes which came to be known as the 'four heads':

- the relief of poverty
- the advancement of education
- the advancement of religion
- other purposes beneficial to the community.[48]

For all of these, it is essential that the purposes are for the 'public benefit' – that is, the benefit of the community or a significant section of it.

So far, so good. The courts still use the 1601 Preamble and the 'four heads' definition as a touchstone, but obviously they realise that times have changed since those days. The needs of society in the 21st century are definitely not reflected closely in those words, after all. So the courts and the Charity Commission can accept new and improved charitable purposes – as long as they are analogous to any existing charitable purpose. This way, they reason, the courts and the Charity Commissioners have managed to get the law to reflect changes in social and economic circumstances. But it's also created a complicated legal framework. It's not hard to see how it can create some surprising situations: some groups that people presume are charities actually aren't, and others which look for all the world like businesses or government agencies are actually registered charities.

For example – while almost all Britons (93 per cent) know that Oxfam is a charity, only one in five knows the Royal Opera House is too. Meanwhile, nearly two out of three think Amnesty International is a charity (no – and we'll see why shortly) and 7 per cent think the Body Shop is (wrong again – it's a limited company).[49]

So how come Eton College, Cambridge University Press and numerous expensive private hospitals can enjoy charitable status – while Amnesty International doesn't? Let's look again at those four heads and consider how the Charity Commission defines them.

The relief of financial hardship

As long as your beneficiaries are in genuine financial need, there's scope for this head to include help for people suffering from the effects of old age, sickness or a disability. It doesn't have to be a long-term financial need. And there are many different ways that charities can relieve hardship:

giving money, providing food, clothing or housing, giving advice or supporting other groups that are helping people in need.

The advancement of education
This doesn't just include schools, colleges or universities – it can also include playgroups, organisations providing work-related training or research institutions. It doesn't include political or 'propagandist' activities, though. Research has to be objective and impartial and made available to the public.

The advancement of religion
There is a general assumption that the advancement of religion is for the public benefit – but in order to qualify as a religion, you've got to have a belief in a supreme being or beings and express that belief through worship. If a religion qualifies, then this head covers provision and upkeep of places of worship, paying ministers or priests and holding services.

'Purposes beneficial to the community'
According to the Charity Commission, a few examples of this are:

- the relief of old age, sickness or disability, where there is no financial need
- promoting racial harmony
- the resettlement and rehabilitation of offenders and drug abusers

- providing help for victims of natural or civil disasters
- promoting human rights
- the provision of recreational facilities which are open to everyone (for example, a sports centre) or which are for particular beneficiary groups such as people with disabilities or the elderly
- urban and rural regeneration and community capacity building
- promotion of health (e.g. through education, access to medical facilities or the pursuit of healthy recreation through sport).

And what about that 'public benefit' requirement?

There will be some causes that fit into one of the four heads above, but still can't be considered charitable because they are not considered to be for the public benefit. A purpose can't be charitable if it's mainly for the benefit of one person or specific individuals. It also can't be charitable if the beneficiaries are somehow related – to the person setting up the charity, perhaps, or where they all hold the same job (although this is less stringently applied when it comes to the financial hardship head – so you could have a charity that catered to hard-up people who had the same employer). A religion would fail the public benefit test if the benefit was completely private (like an entirely enclosed religious order where the only activity is private prayer) or if the organisation's beliefs undermined the accepted foundations of religion and morality.

And finally: no organisation can be charitable if its purposes are illegal or against the public interest, or if it is created for the specific purpose of carrying out political or propagandist aims.

> ### What are some of the more unusual charities out there?
>
> Looking through the Charity Commission's Central Register of Charities, it's immediately clear that although the four heads of charity are pretty clear, they cover a huge range of charitable causes. Here are five lesser-known charities that caught our eye:
>
> *Care, Rehabilitation and Aid for Sick Hedgehogs*
> **Working name: CRASH, CRASH Hedgehog Hospital**
> CRASH's objectives are to relieve suffering and distress of hedgehogs in need of care and attention by providing a rescue, treatment and rehabilitation service for abandoned, neglected or injured hedgehogs; and to advance public education in the study of hedgehogs and in the care, methods of treatment, nursing, conservation and habitat of hedgehogs.
> **www.hedgehogs.org.uk**
> **Tel: 01202 699358**

Ancient Order of Druids – Convalescent Home Fund

This charity aims to provide a period of convalescence and recuperation in an approved and registered convalescent home for a brother of the ancient order of druids or his dependants after illness or accident.
Tel: 01322 289324

The Society of Leather Technologists and Chemists Ltd

The society aims to assist and encourage the application of science and technology to the manufacture and utilisation of leather and related products and to further the development of scientific knowledge in the leather industry.
Tel: 01604 892062

The Lost Musicals Charitable Trust

This charity works to advance the education of the general public in musical theatre by researching and performing 'neglected 20th-century American musicals of historical and educational value'.
Tel: 0207 483 2175

> *The Central Council of Church Bell Ringers Rescue Fund for Redundant Bells*
> 'The object of the fund shall be to advance the Christian religion by the rescue of redundant bells for the purpose of their being rehoused elsewhere for ringing in churches.'
> **Tel: 0208 876 4478**

How are charities regulated?

In England and Wales, the Charity Commission is the body that regulates charities. It requires most charities to register, and those with annual incomes over £10,000 must file their accounts and annual reports each year. Charities which don't do this are placed on a Defaulting Charities list on the Commission's website. The Commission also maintains the Register of Charities, which you can search to find out more about any registered charity.

It's worth noting, though, that a few charities don't have to register with the Commission; very small charities, some places of worship and some religious charities are excepted from registration. Certain other organisations like some educational institutions, friendly societies and national museums have charitable status but are exempt from registering. The Charity Commission's website (www.charity-commission.gov.uk) can help a little more with these definitions.

The Commission gives guidance to charities about the best ways to carry out their aims. And it also has broad legal powers to investigate fraud or dishonesty. Reports of all the Commission's inquiries are published on its website. In Scotland, the Office of the Scottish Charity Regulator has similar powers.

What is the benefit of being a charity? Are there any disadvantages?

As the Charity Commission explains, there are a number of advantages to becoming a registered charity.

Charities can take advantage of a number of tax incentives (worth some £2.8 billion a year to the sector[50]) and pay no more than 20 per cent of normal business rates on the buildings they use. It's easier for them to raise funds from public grant-making trusts and local government. Plus there's the advantage of status: completing the registration process shows that the charity's purposes are in line with the law. Charities are required to work towards their stated aims and represent the people on whose behalf they are working; they can also give their donors the assurance that they are being monitored and advised by the Charity Commission.

But there are some things that charities can't do: for example, they must have exclusively charitable purposes and so there are limits to the kind of political or campaigning activities they can take on. Strict rules apply to how charities can trade and there are also financial reporting requirements.

For these reasons, some groups choose not to operate as charities – and some others aren't allowed to. There are some 500,000 voluntary organisations in the UK, and of those fewer than 200,000 are registered charities.[51]

So which groups don't get charitable status?

Here are a few types of organisations that you might be surprised to hear don't qualify as charities:

- individual sports clubs set up to benefit their members or promote excellence – as opposed to sports facilities open to everyone
- the promotion of political or propagandist purposes, or the promotion of a particular point of view (although there are ways in which charities can promote political ends without falling foul of this – we'll look at this in a moment)
- groups where the people in charge get significant personal benefit
- raising funds for other charities where the organisers don't get any say over how the funds are spent
- purposes which promote friendship or international friendship, like town twinning associations.

Political campaigning – what is and isn't okay

As we've seen above, an organisation that is set up solely for political purposes can't be a charity. But if the prevailing mood among many of the larger charities is that campaigning for change is an integral part of their job – a way to strike at the root causes of the problems they're tackling and an important part of carrying out their strategic aims – then where is the line drawn, and how do charities work around it?

Amnesty International's UK section (AIUK) is not a charity, and indeed for many years it could not have received charitable status. Since its stated aim of improving human rights was, for the most part, achievable only by lobbying governments to change their legislation, this was not considered to be a charitable purpose. So AIUK formed a separate organisation, Amnesty International (UK section) Charitable Trust, to carry out purposes that could be charitable: research into human rights, relief for victims of abuses and work towards the abolition of torture.[52] The Charitable Trust benefits from all the tax advantages given to registered charities, including Gift Aid.

In April 2004 the first steps towards revising this situation were taken in the form of a guidance note from the Charity Commission. The Commission noted that a report by the Government Strategy Unit had recommended that charities should be encouraged to campaign, not dissuaded; their links with local communities and the high level of public trust in charities made them well-placed to offer alternative means of engaging in the political process, while the diversity of causes represented by UK charities meant that a whole range of voices which might normally be lost to mainstream politics could be heard by the government.[53]

The Charity Commission now recognises that while political activity can't be the sole aim of a charity, it's crucial to helping charities achieve their stated aims. For example, international development charities have, within the last couple of decades, become quite actively involved in campaigning about debt relief, aid and international institutions – these issues attempt to strike at the roots of poverty, while other parts of their organisation address the short- and medium-term issues facing people in need.

The Commission's guidelines clarify the position:

- organisations set up to advocate or oppose changes in the law (either in the UK or abroad) or support a political party can't be charities
- organisations set up for charitable purposes can campaign or take part in other political activities
- but trustees of a charity need to make sure that campaigning and politics don't become the sole focus of the charity
- and they also need to consider the benefits (raising public awareness, a change in behaviour or government policy) against the potential risks (losing credibility, compromising independence).[54]

The issue will be further clarified when the new Charities Bill becomes law (we'll discuss this in the next section). At the time of writing, for logistical reasons AIUK does not plan to merge the two parts of its organisation – the non-charitable part will remain so, but more and more of AIUK's work will be able to be done through the charity.[55] But the gains from obtaining charitable status for the whole organisation could be significant – it's thought that if 80 per cent of AIUK's members gave through the Gift Aid scheme, the organisation would be some £2 million better off.

The new Charities Bill

There were high hopes that the new Charities Bill would become law before the 2005 General Election. As it turned out, it was included in the first Queen's Speech after the election and received its first reading in the House of Lords the next day, 18 May 2005. By the time this book is published, it should be enacted. The new Bill is eagerly awaited by the non-profit sector as it represents a chance for change that is long overdue.

The new Bill sets out twelve new charitable purposes which aim to reflect modern-day expectations of charity more closely:

- The prevention and relief of poverty
- The advancement of education
- The advancement of religion (this can include religions which involve belief in more than one god – or none at all)
- The advancement of health
- The advancement of citizenship or community development

- The advancement of arts, heritage or science
- The advancement of amateur sport
- The advancement of human rights, conflict resolution or reconciliation
- The advancement of environmental protection and improvement
- The relief of those in need, by reason of youth, age, ill-health, disability, financial disadvantage or other disadvantage
- The advancement of animal welfare
- Purposes recognised under existing charity law or considered 'analogous' to any of the above.

As well as falling into one of the twelve categories above, an organisation will also have to show that it offers a public benefit. This aspect will continue to be defined and applied by the Charity Commission.

There are other changes in the Bill — clarifying the role and powers of the Commission and setting out its accountability; regulating fundraising and public collections; and some minor changes to laws about registration and financial regulation.

The new bill will apply in England and Wales. Scotland has been going through a parallel process and its bill was passed in June 2005.

The new law will be a boon to the voluntary sector, which has been calling for reform for some time. It will clarify the existing laws and bring them into line with most people's expectations about what charities are and what their roles should be. Some of the changes may mean that existing charities will have to prove their 'public benefit' to keep their status – public schools and private hospitals, for example, will have to show that they benefit the wider public and not just the people who can afford to pay their fees. And the new charitable purposes will mean that groups like Amnesty International and local sports clubs can get the benefits of registration.

But above all, the new laws – in England and the rest of the UK – aim to retain the trust and confidence that the British public have in the voluntary sector. We want our charities to be transparent, effective and in touch with what our society needs. The law changes, as well as the reforms going on within the sector itself, should help keep them that way.

3

Why Should I Give to Charity?

Economic theorists puzzle over the idea of giving to charity – can it really be human instinct? Otherwise, why would we work so hard to earn money only to give it away?

It seems like a really obvious reason, but here goes: people give to charities because they think it's a good thing to do. And it's a good thing to do because charities do good work. They help to make the world a better, safer, fairer place. And most of us, however selfish we might be normally, acknowledge that a fairer world is something we should all be aiming for.

But what other reasons might there be for supporting charity? First of all, giving to charity enables you as an individual to effect real change. Each year charities spend £20.4 billion in furthering their aims in the UK. The sector employs more than half a million people and contributes £7.2 billion to the UK gross domestic product.[56] If charities weren't in the picture, there would be £580 million less to spend on cancer research, £363 million less for environmental and heritage causes, £271 million less for animal protection.[57]

Working on our own, very few of us have the skills or the money to make any meaningful contribution in some of these areas. But collectively, all of us can help to fund research to find a cure for cancer, raise awareness of child abuse or provide search-and-rescue services – to name but a few causes. By giving to charity and pooling our money and support with others, our donations become very powerful.

Charity is an important element of all modern societies – Britain included. Imagine a world that consisted only of the public (government) and private (business) sectors. Imagine no one picking up those who fell through the enormous rift between these two giant forces. Charity can help to supplement areas where the state just can't provide for those who need it. Without it, the state would struggle to cope with the 380,000 Britons who are sleeping rough or in temporary accommodation.[58] There would be far fewer refuges for women in abusive relationships to seek shelter for themselves and their children. And international organisations would be forced to rely on government aid to help victims of natural disasters. Currently more than 40 per cent of social services in the UK – such as home care, shelters for the homeless, addiction treatment services and respite programmes – are run by charities.[59]

Charities don't just scramble to pick up the pieces, either. The Charity Commission and the courts have recently acknowledged that campaigning work is an integral part of how charities achieve their stated aims – for example, relieving poverty is not just a matter of helping particular families buy things they need, it's also about campaigning for ways to reduce the inequalities and barriers that keep people in poverty. Charities have the contacts and the influence to talk to the people in charge and put pressure on them to make changes.

Some charities rely solely on funding from the government and various other grant-making bodies – they do no public fundraising. But most charities need money from individual donations, both to keep doing their existing work and to keep pushing for change. Government is playing an increasing role in funding the charity sector and it's estimated that around a third of the income of general household charities comes from the British government – some £5 billion.[60] But obviously this raises a number of issues: about how much the government will use charities to give its social welfare policies legitimacy in the eyes of the public, and about how much charities will be able to criticise the government if they rely on it for the majority of their funding. Donations from the public help to reduce a charity's reliance on this kind of funding, helping it to maintain a healthy independence.

Through charity, we support each other by pledging our time and money to our community and our society. At its best, it helps break down the barriers between rich and poor, have and have-not, just a little bit. The current government believes that giving to charity, volunteering and other means of supporting the not-for-profit sector are very important because they help to build social cohesion, forging links within communities and helping people to get the things they need. Two years after coming to power, the Prime Minister Tony Blair addressed the national conference of the National Council for Voluntary Organisations (NCVO) and spelt out his vision:

> What does it say about the country we became in the late 20th century that do-gooding, rather than being the foundation stone of the fair society and vibrant communities that we want, became a term of abuse? It is good to do good. Good for those charities and organisations and neighbourhoods in which the good is being done. But good for the do-gooder as well.[61]

But in what way *is* giving to charity 'good for the do-gooder'? What does the giver get out of it? Why is philanthropy such an enduring human tradition?

Some people believe that giving to charity is some kind of instinct, developed because it benefits our species in some way. At first, this seems like a strange idea: Darwin's theories of evolution presume that individuals should act to preserve their *own* interests, not those of the species as a whole. But the British evolutionary biologist Richard Dawkins believes that natural selection has given us the ability to feel pity for someone who is suffering. When humans lived in small clan-based groups, a person in need would be a relative or someone who could pay you back a good turn later, so taking pity on others could benefit you in the long run. Modern societies are much less close-knit and when we see a heartfelt appeal for charity, chances are we may never even meet the person who is suffering – but the emotion of pity is still in our genes.[62]

There are even signs that we humans may be embarrassed by our own generosity – to the extent that people may give more willingly if they can pretend it's not a purely altruistic act. One recent study found that when asked to give to a highly worthy cause (a group to help emotionally disturbed children) the donation rate trebled if donors were offered a gift in return for their money; but when asked to give to a mildly worthy cause (a softball team) the gift made no difference.[63]

This study, carried out in the US, echoes the words of the French philosopher Alexis de Tocqueville:

> Americans enjoy explaining almost every act of their lives on the principle of self-interest. It gives them great pleasure to point out how an enlightened self-love continually leads them to help one another and disposes them freely to give part of their time and wealth for the good of the state. They do themselves less than justice, for sometimes in the United States, as elsewhere, one sees people carried away by the spontaneous impulses natural to man. But the Americans are hardly prepared to admit that they do give way to emotions of this sort.[64]

Those words were written more than 150 years ago but it's interesting to consider them today. It's hard to see British charity donors talking about their 'enlightened self-love'. But since it benefits human beings to live in a benign world, it follows that we should get substantial satisfaction from making the world a better place. And giving to charity does benefit society. People often say they feel happy about giving money to a needy cause and there is much talk about a 'warm glow'. We give money and time to help other people not because we expect any favours in return but because we are glad to have done something.

4

Why Do People Say I Shouldn't Give to Charity?

It's an expression my dad uses sometimes, and it has a distinctly Victorian ring about it: 'cold as charity'.

It's probably true to say that in the past charity could be a particularly chill and unwelcome thing to receive. As far back as Tudor times, a distinction was made between 'the deserving poor' – those who wanted to work but couldn't find jobs, or who were too old or sick to support themselves – and 'the undeserving poor'. Those who deserved it would receive support and charity; those who did not would be whipped and driven away.

In 1853 Charles Dickens painted a cruel little portrait of this kind of philanthropist in his book *Bleak House*:

> Mr Jarndyce had fallen into this company [of men with charitable missions], in the tenderness of his heart and his earnest desire to do all the good in his power; but, that he felt it to be too often an unsatisfactory company, where benevolence took spasmodic forms; where charity was

assumed, as a regular uniform, by loud professors and speculators in cheap notoriety, vehement in profession, restless and vain in action, servile in the last degree of meanness to the great, adulatory of one another, and intolerable to those who were anxious quietly to help the weak from failing, rather than with a great deal of bluster and self-laudation to raise them up a little way when they were down.[65]

Gifts also came with substantial strings attached. Those who were lucky enough to receive charity had to abide by high standards of morality and self-improvement – they were required to 'better themselves', on the terms of their givers.

No less a commentator than Oscar Wilde was moved to write about the problems of Victorian approaches to charity – and the fact that some people's motivations for giving might be less than ideal. In his essay 'The Soul of Man under Socialism', he set out the damage that he felt charity did to society:

> The majority of people spoil their lives by an unhealthy and exaggerated altruism – are forced, indeed, so to spoil them. They find themselves surrounded by hideous poverty, by hideous ugliness, by hideous starvation ... Accordingly, with admirable, though misdirected intentions, they very seriously and very sentimentally set themselves to the task of remedying the evils that they see. But their remedies do not cure the disease: they merely prolong it. Indeed, their remedies are part of the disease.

> They try to solve the problem of poverty, for instance, by keeping the poor alive; or, in the case of a very advanced school [of thought], by amusing the poor.
>
> But this is not a solution: it is an aggravation of the difficulty. The proper aim is to try and reconstruct society on such a basis that poverty will be impossible. And the altruistic virtues have really prevented the carrying out of this aim. Just as the worst slave-owners were those who were kind to their slaves, and so prevented the horror of the system being realised by those who suffered from it, and understood by those who contemplated it, so, in the present state of things in England, the people who do most harm are the people who try to do most good; and at last we have had the spectacle of men who have really studied the problem and know the life – educated men who live in the East End – coming forward and imploring the community to restrain its altruistic impulses of charity, benevolence, and the like. They do so on the ground that such charity degrades and demoralises. They are perfectly right. Charity creates a multitude of sins.[66]

So what exactly does this 'multitude of sins' consist of? What are some of the arguments people put forward against giving to charity, and how can you make sure you don't fall into their trap?

'It's patronising'

One of the meanings of the word 'patronise' is to sponsor or support someone – and in some ways that's what charity does. But a more common meaning of the word is to condescend to someone – graciously lowering yourself to their level, slumming it – and, by implication, belittling them. It's this aspect of charity which is often criticised.

Patronising charity creates a relationship whereby the donor can see themselves as generous and full of pity – and the receiver must be slavishly grateful for any contribution. The giver considers the needy person as somehow inferior to themselves, and the receiver is locked into a cycle of dependence.

But it doesn't have to be that way. If we give in a mindful and involved fashion – thinking not just about helping someone 'deserving', someone 'less lucky than we are', but about the causes of the problems and what we can do about them – then that's a huge leap on from Victorian cold charity.

Donors in rich countries also need to recognise that the person who's on the receiving end may see things differently. What we might see as straightforward, non-judgemental acts of charity may look quite different to the recipient.

This is an important issue for the non-profit sector, and charities and other voluntary groups do seek to address this in formulating strategy. Rather than just giving money passively, many organisations try to get donors involved in the process of change – encouraging people to become involved in activist work, letter-writing campaigns and the like. Some non-governmental organisations (NGOs) talk about adopting an approach that's based on human rights. In practice this means international groups will work closely with grass-roots organisations in poor countries – the local groups concentrate on delivering aid money where it's needed and the international organisation will help them get what they're entitled to.

Building relationships and furthering understanding of the issues involved is important too. One senior NGO manager says it's really important for potential donors to think hard about the charities they give to – perhaps giving larger amounts to a smaller number of organisations and really engaging with these groups.

At the Live8 concert in London's Hyde Park in July 2005, U2's Bono told a worldwide audience: 'We're not looking for charity; we're looking for justice.' This is something of a rallying cry for the modern non-profit sector and it echoes the words of Mary Wollstonecraft, the women's rights campaigner and reformer who wrote in 1790:

> ... true happiness arises from the friendship and intimacy which can only be enjoyed by equals; and charity is not a condescending distribution of alms, but an intercourse of good offices and mutual benefits, founded on respect for justice and humanity.[67]

At its best, charity will seek to build some kind of solidarity between the giver and receiver. It will create relationships. Perhaps it will go beyond the straightforward donor–donee relationship – perhaps both sides will get so much from their contact that it'll be hard to say who gives and who receives. And when both sides can work together to achieve social change that strikes at the heart of problems – that's the ultimate.

Dr Augustus Jessop was a cleric and writer who, towards the end of the Victorian era, examined the problem of providing housing for the rural poor. He sums up what we should be aiming for rather nicely:

> [These efforts must] come from philanthropists who are not ambitious of doing things in the grand style; who have no desire to sound a trumpet before them on the one hand nor to do good by deputy and send a big cheque to some society on the other. What they give they must give with gentle, warm, loving, living, not with cold, bloodless and often very cruel, dead hand.[68]

'It's just a way for rich people to smugly absolve themselves of any responsibility'

It's probably true that there are some people who give a little bit of money to charity and then think that they've done all they need to do. To take one recent and well-publicised example, there are plenty of people who bought the Band Aid 20 single who didn't understand the complex political structures that allowed the crisis in Darfur to come about.

Unfortunately, it's also very easy for critics of particular events or charities to brand them as smug or irresponsible.

Even more unfortunately, these tend to be the kinds of stories picked up by certain parts of the media. Look at the storm of criticism that accompanied the announcement of the line-up for the Live8 concert in July 2005. While the event attracted many millions of viewers and focused the world's attention on rich countries' failure to make a real commitment to Africa, some music industry insiders criticised the organiser Bob Geldof for not including more African musicians. One record label executive accused Geldof of 'talk[ing] about fair trade for Africa, but he's acting just like the West when it comes to choosing who will appear. He said that he wanted to tilt the world a bit in favour of the poor and Africa, and he's missed a golden opportunity to do just that.'[69] By not recognising African artists, the argument went, the rich donors will be able to give their money while not really thinking about the ways in which they and their governments might perpetuate the situation.

There have also been many, many column inches dedicated to the phenomenon of the charity wristband. At the time of writing, they were still a hot fashion item, but by the time you read this they may be deeply uncool. When charities flirt with trends, they run the risk of people adopting their cause for the wrong reasons – and as fashions wane, so too may income for the causes that sought to take advantage.

It's probably true that some people didn't think long and hard about why they queued for Live8 tickets or an anti-racism wristband. But there are plenty more who did, and part of a charity's work includes making donors aware of the issues.

There's also a danger that we might think just giving money is enough – and overlook some of the things that we could do in our own lives to make a change. In a recent report, the British think-tank Civitas proposed that ours has become a society that cares too much: rather than doing something concrete about a problem, we would sooner wear a ribbon, sign an internet petition or observe a minute's silence. Civitas believes this shows that Britain is not becoming more altruistic, but more selfish. We do these things not to do good, but to feel good.[70]

Robert Whelan of Civitas set out the report's rallying cry: 'Turn off the television, get off your backside, go out and do something, talk to a homeless person, do something, but don't tell us all what a nice person you are by making these hollow gestures.'[71]

While this does seem like an overly harsh assessment of people's motivations in giving to charity, it's worth thinking about. Buying a ribbon, a button or a charity record is certainly helping the cause you're supporting. It's not tokenism – the red ribbon for HIV/Aids has not just helped to raise money, it's also done a huge amount to raise awareness and fight prejudice.

But the danger is that people will stop there, thinking that the act of buying a white band will be enough to Make Poverty History, when of course it isn't. Don't just wear a ribbon – in fact don't just give money – get out into your community and make a real difference.

'It doesn't solve the root causes of the problems it sets out to alleviate'

Some charities actively set out to solve root causes, others don't. It's not wrong for some charities to concentrate on alleviating short-term problems. If there's a natural disaster that's left people starving, then those are the charities that will send emergency food and medical care. Others will work on longer-term projects like reconstruction, solutions for dealing with displaced people and reconciliation. Medical charities may choose to focus on helping people who have fallen prey to a disease or to fund research into the causes of that disease.

There are other areas that are less straightforward. Many of the problems facing developing countries – and developed countries, for that matter – are to do with poverty. This is not just an economic issue, it's a political issue as well, and unless the global community can make a serious effort at tackling the inequalities that exist in the modern world, things will continue to get worse. The gap between rich and poor is widening, not just on a global level, but within societies as well.

So charities have a role to play here both in the short term – providing families and communities with farming equipment and crops to enable them to feed themselves, for example – and in the longer term, putting pressure on governments and corporations to change the way they work with the developing world, and working with grass-roots groups who are helping to empower local people.

If you're really concerned about attacking the root causes of some of these issues, then there are other things you can do. At a private level, you can volunteer in your local community, encourage environmental initiatives at home, in your workplace and in your borough, write letters to prisoners of conscience, buy fairly traded food and products. At a national level, you can join in the movements that are trying to get governments to tackle issues seriously and sincerely.

At the time of writing, there is a huge groundswell forming around the issue of debt relief. The developing world now spends $13 on debt repayment for every $1 it receives in grants and aid.[72] Just think what could happen if those repayments could be spent on development projects. And if the rich world were to remove the vast system of agricultural subsidies (currently costing $1 billion every day), it would help too – because for every $1 poor countries receive in aid, they lose $2 due to unfair trade barriers against their goods.[73] If some of these issues are tackled honestly, then developing countries can make real progress.

There are charities and other voluntary groups out there tackling the root causes of all these issues – and if that is where you'd like to see your money go, get out there and support them. Remember: charity is good, but change is even better.

'Most of the money doesn't go where it's needed because charities spend a lot more money on administration and big salaries than they ought to'

Why does one aid agency pay its staff an average salary of £3,400 per year – while a health research group pays more than £44,000? How can the Citizens' Advice Bureau spend 2p per £1 it raises on administration – while the Samaritans spend 29p?[74] And why did it take a court decision to suspend the accounts of a Scottish breast cancer charity when it was revealed that only £1.5 million of the £13 million it had raised went to charitable causes?[75]

The release of a charity 'league table' in early 2005 aimed to point out that some charities spend more than others on administration and salaries. The company's website warns the public: 'Find out which [charities] are excellent at keeping costs down and which ones are hopeless!'[76]

Doesn't this reveal that some charities are spending a lot more money on themselves than on the people they're trying to help? Well, not necessarily.

For a start, the league tables don't compare like with like. Different kinds of charities have different aims – and some of those aims may take a lot more money to pursue. At first glance, the Royal Society for the Protection of Birds might seem to have quite high wage costs. But that's because many of its specialist staff are out in the field actively pursuing the organisation's aims.

It might not even be that meaningful to compare two charities working in the same field. Look at international development charities, for instance: some work directly in the field, while others choose to co-ordinate with local partners on the ground. The charity that works directly may spend more on administration, but that's because local partners will be shouldering much of the admin bill for the latter charity.[77]

Secondly, some charitable campaigns seek to raise awareness rather than raise funds directly. The National Society for the Prevention of Cruelty to Children's 'Full Stop' campaign had high initial fundraising costs, but a very strong educational impact.[78] Similarly, the Terrence Higgins Trust works not only to help people living with HIV and Aids, but also to raise public awareness – which inevitably costs more.

It's also not uncommon for charities to get separate funding for administration, or to operate under the umbrella of another, larger group which provides a management infrastructure. These charities might appear to have very low admin costs (or none at all) but the fact is, they're still paying – it's just that they've raised the money another way.[79]

Charities need to work in different ways to raise funds, too. Legacy fundraising – where charities encourage people to make gifts in their wills – has very low cost ratios, and this benefits the types of charities that traditionally attract a lot of legacies (like medical charities). It's also true that some popular charities attract donations with very little effort, while others have to work a lot harder – so it may be unfair to compare admin costs for a charity for a popular cause with one that's less popular.

The issue of salaries for charity workers is a thorny one. In the past, people did often selflessly dedicate their lives to charity, working for little or no money – and in smaller charities, many people still do that. But among the top charities today, the reality is a little different. The *Guardian*'s annual salary survey looks at the top 100 charities in Britain and in 2003 it found that the average salary for a charity chief executive was £79,805. The highest-paid charity CEO was Tony Hall of the Royal Opera House Covent Garden, who earned a salary of £205,000.[80]

That does seem like a lot of money and the Association of Chief Executives of Voluntary Organisations (Acevo) acknowledges that pay is still a sensitive issue. But the CEO of Acevo, Stephen Bubb, points out that today's charities are no longer headed by people with huge private incomes. As voluntary sector groups start to operate more and more like businesses – and businesses with substantial budgets and complex structures, at that – they need to recruit professional managers who are experienced and knowledgeable. Charities are having to offer more competitive salaries to attract the best people and a charity staffed with well-paid specialists should be better placed to achieve its long-term aims.

If a charity spends very little on fundraising, salaries and administration, that may not actually be a good thing: it may mean it's not investing enough in its own infrastructure and that it isn't paying competitive salaries to attract the best people. Both of these factors will affect that charity's ability to achieve its long-term goals. But on the other hand, administration costs have to be kept under control.

The Charities Aid Foundation estimates that across the top 500 charities in the UK, around 13–14 per cent of total expenditure goes on fundraising, management and admin.[81] If your chosen charity is spending a lot more (or indeed a lot less) than that, start asking a few questions. What is the charity doing that necessitates higher admin costs than the average and how does that expenditure help them meet their goals? And how do their administration costs compare with other groups doing similar work in the same sector? A dig around the charity's website may tell you all you need to know.

'All charity does is plug the gaps in society – and that's the government's job'

In the direct aftermath of the tsunami in South-East Asia, it soon became clear that people around the world were giving more to help the relief effort than they ever had. But, strangely, it took their governments some time to catch up.

The UN Undersecretary-General for Humanitarian Affairs, Jan Egeland, raised hackles in the American media when he accused the governments of rich countries of being 'stingy'. In a press briefing on 27 December 2004 he was asked whether state aid to the stricken countries in South-East Asia could undercut the UN's relief efforts elsewhere. Egeland replied:

> It is really a problem that for too many rich countries, the pie is finite. You take out a slice and there is less for the rest. And I think an unprecedented disaster like this one should lead to unprecedented generosity from countries that should be new and additional funds, because I wouldn't want to see many of our friends, the donor countries, depleting their natural disaster coffers the first two weeks of January and have nothing more when we come to other disasters ...
>
> We were more generous when we were less rich, many of the rich countries. And it is beyond me why are we so stingy, really ... Christmas time should remind many Western countries at least how rich we have become. And if actually the foreign assistance of many countries now is 0.1 or 0.2 percent of their gross national income, I think that is stingy, really. I don't think that is very generous.

Of course, certain media organisations took this to be a criticism of the US government – but Egeland was extending his criticism more widely, hitting out at countries where foreign assistance falls far short of the figure of 0.7 per cent of GDP set by the UN.

Egeland's comments highlight the relationship between private giving and government spending. He was obviously talking about international aid – but these issues are just as important on a domestic level. Most people in Britain feel that the government has a responsibility to fund good works, but many of them also give to charities themselves. And surveys into British social attitudes show that around 65 per cent of the population feels that the more people give to charity, the less the government will spend – and that somehow giving to charity lets the government off the hook.[82]

Charities have often acted as a kind of back-up system for the state – and indeed, that's been the case since Elizabethan times (as we saw in Chapter 1). Even though Britain and other European countries now have a relatively strong social security structure, there are still areas where the state can't provide and charities have adapted to this new role. As populations in rich countries age and the demands on the state grow accordingly, charities will become even more important in filling in the gaps.

Indeed, the British government is starting to realise the key role that the voluntary sector has in giving support and legitimacy to its social policies. In particular, the Blair government seems very interested in the idea of charity and volunteering as ways to build community and strengthen society. Prime Minister Tony Blair set out his vision to the NCVO annual conference:

> In the first half of this century we learnt that the community cannot achieve its aims without the help of govern-

ment providing essential services, and a backd
ity. In the second half of the century we learnt
ment cannot achieve its aims without the ene
mitment of others – voluntary organisations, busi..._,
and, crucially, the wider public.[83]

The government is increasingly working with charities and it's estimated that a third of the income of household charities now comes from government grants.[84]

But this raises another important issue about the relationship between government and the voluntary sector. In the past, charities have been unafraid to speak out stridently against government policy – and indeed some groups like Amnesty International have deliberately chosen to forgo charitable status so that this kind of campaigning could be their sole focus (as we saw in Chapter 2). As governments and charities move closer together – both in terms of funding and in strategic partnerships – there is the risk that this role may be compromised. Charities may feel less able to speak out against government policy if they know that's where their money is coming from.

This is a difficult issue for charities, and it's one that is worth exploring before you give. How concerned are you about the level of government funding and co-operation, and what do you expect them to be able to do? A quick search of a charity's website should tell you how much of their funding comes in the form of government grants – and if it doesn't, call the charity and ask for a copy of their annual accounts (we'll look at how to do this in the next chapter).

Of course it may be that, given the type of work your charity is doing, co-operation with government is not a real issue. And even if it seems as though your chosen charity isn't speaking out enough, this may be part of some long-term strategic aim. It's worth bearing in mind the words of Stuart Etherington of the NCVO: 'It may be that in some partnerships we trade an independence to criticise or lobby in order to increase our actual influence and ensure better outcomes overall for our users or members.'[85]

'Charities end up getting too involved in politics, and I don't think that's right'

Following on from the point about government funding, what should charities do when carrying out their work might lead them into taking a political stance – or when their work makes them look as if they're on one side or another of a particular debate?

In November 2003 it was revealed that Save the Children UK had been ordered by its US wing to end its criticism of the military action in Iraq. Save the Children UK had accused coalition forces in Iraq of breaching the Geneva Convention by blocking aid. The *Guardian* newspaper saw e-mails from the US branch of the charity which said the statement was 'undermining all the great work we've done ... we'll have to see the consequences of how this plays out – including affecting our future funding from the government'.[86]

More recently the charity Oxfam came under the magnifying glass. An article in the *New Statesman* magazine in May 2005 wondered if the organisation had become too close to the Labour government. The article pointed at Oxfam's leading role in the Make Poverty History campaign and New Labour's keenness to be closely identified with it. It also highlighted areas where Oxfam seemed closely aligned with the government's policies – particularly its Make Trade Fair campaign, which promotes market liberalisation and removal of trade barriers as a key mechanism for reducing poverty. And it queried whether NGOs can work effectively inside the system without losing their independence.[87]

Oxfam defended its position, pointing out that it has not shied away from criticising the Labour government when its policies have been lacking. Oxfam's director Barbara Stocking pointed out that in her view, 'a major campaigning organisation cannot choose between direct lobbying on the "inside" and activism "outside"; each is essential'.[88]

Asked about the Save the Children situation, Britain's charities minister Fiona Mactaggart denied that governments expect charities to toe their line.

> I am absolutely certain that charities and voluntary organisations must have the right to make the case that they think proper ... The thing that I like about charities and

voluntary organisations is that they have a real sense of where the shoe is rubbing, where some bit of policy is causing problems to a group who they care about, and they use that insight to comment on public policy. And I think that's right. It doesn't mean that I agree with them. But I think it's right that we have a better society if they are able to do that.[89]

In an international context, the impartiality of a particular charity or other aid organisation is key to its credibility. Some groups do have a particular focus or take a particular stance, and they're usually fairly easy to spot. But in other cases, NGOs and aid organisations walk a difficult line. Their campaigning work means they have to take sides to a certain extent – they're on the side of the people who are being oppressed.

But there are certainly cases where governments have manipulated NGOs to their own ends. Aid expert David Rieff argues that the failure of the original Live Aid appeal to appreciate the political dimension to the famine in Ethiopia allowed the government of Mengistu Haile Mariam to use Western donors' money to continue their radical reforms in the country – which had contributed to the famine in the first place. Live Aid certainly achieved much, but it may have cost lives as well.[90]

Privately, some NGOs admit that there are times when they have to compromise. They do have to temper their criticisms of governments occasionally in order to protect their workers and partners on the ground – and to maintain contact and influence with those governments. Even when they do speak out, some people will try to make it look like they're taking sides in order to lower the credibility of the charity.

For example, international aid charities have spoken out in the past about the situation in Zimbabwe; recently Action Aid called for major reform to the system of governance in the country so that it could resolve its social and economic crisis.[91] But the organisation says it's also aware of the difficulties of speaking out: the need to protect the safety and security of its workers, the possibility that in some people's minds, it might seem to be taking a position that is pro-colonialist.[92]

Other NGOs, though, are adamant that for them, compromise is not an option. Amnesty International says that at times it may choose to raise concerns with governments first and to give them an opportunity to respond before going public – but that ultimately it puts all its concerns on the public record.

Amnesty has in the past been criticised for its perceived lack of impartiality, particularly in its work on Israel and Palestine. Kristyan Benedict, the campaigns co-ordinator for Amnesty's UK section, explains:

> AI's work on Israel/Occupied Territories is based on international law and on the same principles and policies on which we base our work in the rest of the world.

> [For example], many are critical of AI's position in favour of the right to return for refugees and displaced people in the case of Palestinian refugees. However, AI's position is the same for refugees/displaced people everywhere, including Israel/Palestine.
>
> Many are critical of AI's non-position on occupation in the case of Israel's occupation of the West Bank and Gaza Strip; however, AI does not take a position on occupation anywhere and hence not in the case of Israel/OT either.[93]

Amnesty says that it deals with criticisms of its work in this area in the same way as any other criticism: that is, if the criticisms are about concrete facts, mistakes or erroneous claims, they are addressed. But Kristyan Benedict notes that so far, for the criticisms Amnesty has faced, 'that has not really been the case'.[94]

It is important to be impartial in the sense that charities shouldn't become aligned with a particular political party or administration. But most charities admit that when it comes to working for people who need them, being neutral and blinkered helps no one. They say speaking out and taking the side of people who are oppressed is exactly what they *should* be doing.

'There are so many scams around'

In January 2005 the US Federal Bureau of Investigation issued a warning about scam artists who were attempting to profit from the huge number of people who felt moved to help the victims of the tsunami in South-East Asia. It advised people against giving money to organisations that contacted them via unsolicited e-mail asking them to donate to the relief effort. Similar cons were reported in the UK, too.

Some tsunami scammers pretended to be acting on behalf of established charities, creating websites that looked similar to the genuine article. Others used the technique known as 'phishing' – scammers send out an e-mail which pretends to be from a legitimate organisation (like a bank or, in these cases, a charity) asking people to enter their bank or credit card details into a fake internet site and then stealing money from them. Another e-mail method encourages people to visit internet sites which, when opened, load 'spyware' programs onto their computer. The scammers can then log in to the victim's computer and use the spyware programs to access confidential information stored there.

There were also reports that bogus websites had lured British volunteers to Thailand, ostensibly to work on relief projects – only to have their cash and travel documents taken by fraudsters posing as charity workers. One legitimate charity working to co-ordinate volunteers in Thailand said it had sheltered 'a number' of young Britons who had fallen victim to similar scams. According to Bridget Shank of the Tsunami Volunteer Centre at Khao Lak, 'lots of organisations have sprung up here and it can be hard to tell who's genuine'.[95]

It's outrageous that some dishonest people seek to

make money from other people's generosity – but it's something that you need to watch out for. In May 2005 three men in California's Bay Area were jailed after scamming more than $3 million in donations to fictitious charities. They set up call centres pretending to be collecting for police benevolent funds and youth charities – over seven years they collected some $3.6 million, of which just $50,000 was given to charity.[96]

Other kinds of donations may be susceptible to scams, too. In 2004 the UK Office of Fair Trading warned the British public to be wary of bogus charity clothing collections. Typically, scammers would leave flyers in letterboxes asking people to donate unwanted clothes, footwear and household items to poor families in Eastern Europe or developing countries. The flyers suggest that the items are being collected for charity, but they're actually being organised by commercial operators who sell the clothes at a profit. It's estimated that charity shops could be losing out on over £1 million of goods each year.[97]

Even the much-publicised charity wristband can be a way for scammers to make money. The famous yellow Livestrong bracelets promoted by cyclist Lance Armstrong to raise awareness of testicular cancer change hands on the internet for as much as £5, and the BBC's Newsround programme found fake charity wristbands for sale in several shops. Needless to say, the bands look like the genuine article, but the money goes straight into the pockets of the people selling them.[98]

The good news is that there are a few simple steps you can take to avoid falling prey to scammers. Give smart and do a little bit of research. Take extra care when you're giving on the internet. And don't ever be afraid to ask for credentials, proof of how money is spent or contact details to find out more information: any legitimate charity will be more than happy to help you. We'll examine some more scam-busting tips in the next chapter.

'I give through the National Lottery. Isn't that enough?'

Certainly, giving to charity through buying a lottery ticket is a good option. Out of every £1 spent on the National Lottery, about 28p goes to what it calls 'Good Causes'. These are laid out under five broad categories – arts, charities, heritage, 'health, education and the environment' and sports.

Since the Lottery began in 1994, it's raised some £17 billion for the Good Causes.[99] Fourteen bodies are responsible for distributing funds – and although the grants are made in accordance with government guidelines, they are independent. All the same, lottery grants have come in for the inevitable media criticism. For example, one newspaper encouraged its readers to write to the Community Fund and 'vent their anger' over a grant of £340,000 to a group which helped asylum seekers fight deportation.[100] A survey two years later showed that the public were largely confused about how lottery cash was given out, with most overestimating the amount of money that went to groups helping asylum seekers.[101]

At the time of writing, a bill to reform the National Lottery was before the House of Commons – and this would give the public more say in where lottery money is spent. If it's passed in its current form, it will give distributors the power to consult and take into account the public's views when deciding whether to make a grant.

So a lottery ticket does help charity and the 180,000 projects that have been funded since 1994 are no doubt very happy that you play. And then, of course, there's the chance of winning a large amount of money – which, it has to be said, charities don't offer. But if you really want to have some control over where your money goes and what causes you'd like to support, you'd be better off making a direct donation as well.

'I give spare change to beggars because I feel bad saying no. Why should I give to homelessness charities as well?'

It is hard to say no when someone asks you for spare change – particularly if it's a cold rainy night and you're on your way home to a warm house and a good dinner. It's just a pound to you, after all, whereas to them it might mean a cup of tea or something to eat, or it could help them find a hostel bed for the night.

This is a tricky ethical dilemma. There are many charities

in the UK working to help homeless people – Crisis, Shelter and the Big Issue Foundation are among them. They not only work to help individual homeless people and families find places to stay, but also lobby government for action on housing issues. They provide opportunities to learn skills and get support or treatment for addiction or mental health problems, and they work with the housing sector to help people at risk. Among other projects, Crisis runs practical and creative workshops for homeless people and gives grants to help people get training and set up businesses, while Shelter runs a network of Housing Aid centres and helps to resettle families into new accommodation.

If you give money to an individual beggar, they might indeed spend it on a hot meal or a place to sleep. Or they might not. There have been many reports of gangs in Britain's cities employing people to beg on their behalf. To give just one example, in 2004 a court in Leeds heard how a group of eight beggars in the city made up to £90,000 a year.[102] And although some of these stories play on deeper, more divisive issues than homelessness – fears about asylum seekers and immigration, in other words – they do illustrate that your money won't always go where you expect. And even if gangs are an exception rather than a rule, your kindness might inadvertently help support local drug dealers and other petty crime. You can't give money to a beggar and then tell them how to spend it – so you have to accept the risk that your spare change, however well-intentioned, may not help that person at all.

Ultimately, this is a decision that you have to make yourself – would you rather help one homeless person on one occasion, or contribute to a larger effort to tackle the root causes of homelessness and empower people to make their own lives better? It's a tough call. Sometimes it's very hard to say no. But if you want to make a real difference with that spare change, then a donation to charity can be the best way to achieve that.

'It's totally undemocratic!'

In one way, you could think of charitable giving as the ultimate democratic act – you and only you decide where to give your money and which causes are important to you. But as we saw in Chapter 1, if we are indeed at the start of a golden age of philanthropy, then there will be a lot of people out there with a lot more money than you – and very clear ideas about how they want to spend it.

If the whole population gives to charity, then the patterns of charitable giving should reflect what the whole population wants to fund. When you look at the overall levels of support for the different charity sectors, it's clear to see what Britain cares about most: medical research, and children and young people. Religion and the arts come further down the list. But compare the causes supported by 'elite givers' – those who give £50 or more a month. Almost half of elite givers support religious charities (compared with just over 10 per cent of other givers) and two other sectors fare disproportionately well – international aid, and culture, arts and music (see table overleaf). As one senior NGO worker says wryly, there is a great propensity for the super-rich to give to causes where their name might end up on an art gallery or a theatre.

Given that many commentators predict an increase in the number of super-rich philanthropists, especially in the US, this imbalance is likely to continue. Nearly two-thirds of the money given to charity in the US goes to religious causes now[103] – how will that change if more and more money is going to private grant-making foundations, whose benefactors will have clear ideas of where they want their money to go?

The new Charity Bill may help to redress some of this concern with its insistence on a 'public benefit' test. This will be a mandatory requirement for all charities, regardless of which category they fall into – and it's possible that wealthy and relatively exclusive organisations like private schools and hospitals could lose their charitable status if they can't demonstrate that they benefit the public.

Charities are resigned to the idea that there are some causes that will always attract big donations from very wealthy people – and that there are other causes which will always seem less attractive to a certain kind of donor. But that's not always a bad thing. Melvin Coleman, the finance director of Amnesty UK, says that AI doesn't mind being reliant on a lot of 'ordinary' donors. The vast majority of us, after all, are not so vulnerable to stock market crashes, tax

Patterns of giving among elite givers vs. other givers

Cause	Proportion supporting each cause (%)		Mean amount given (£)	
	Elite givers	Other givers	Elite givers	Other givers
Religion	43.4	10.8	22.03	0.60
Children and young people	43.3	21.2	20.58	0.88
International aid	29.9	8.5	13.06	0.40
Heritage	7.8	0.8	1.88	0.02
Culture, arts and music	5.4	0.8	1.39	0.04

Source: NCVO/NOP 2000, taken from *A Lot of Give*, Charities Aid Foundation, 2002.

laws and other things that affect rich givers. And, as he puts it, there is great strength in having 200,000 donors all giving £5 a month.[104] The very fact that you give your support, regardless of the amount, means that there is a big mandate for that organisation to do its work – and ultimately, that is the real democracy.

So what's the conclusion?

A lot of the arguments against giving to charity boil down to issues of trust: whether we believe that charities are doing a good job, whether we think they're spending our money wisely, whether they are transparent enough in the way they operate. If charities are accepting a lot of money from big business and government, then how can their donors be sure that they're still able to do their job properly?

Some critics also have a lot to say about the kind of people who give to charity. The old arguments about the relationships of dependence created between generous rich-world donors and grateful poor-world recipients are still as true as they ever were, and others point to the supposed smugness of people who give a small amount of money to a particular cause and feel they've done enough to absolve themselves of any responsibility.

One thing that you can do to start resolving some of these issues is get more involved in your charity giving. If you're concerned about perpetuating the Victorian stereotype of gracious philanthropy, then get more involved with your chosen charities – find out more about their ethos and their work, see if there are other more personal ways you can become involved in helping them reach their goals. Think about supporting charities that are involved in campaigning work as well as those that are working to alleviate an immediate crisis.

If you're already an established giver or are considering

your options, then take the time to find out more about your chosen charities. Are you happy that they're getting the most out of your donations, and if not, what should you do about it? Do you think your charity is being as independent and honest with you as it should be? In the next chapter, we'll look at how you can go about finding out more about charities, their financial structures and their reputations.

5

OK, So I Want to Give – How?

Being smart about charity giving means considering all the different ways that you could give and deciding what suits you best. It means making sure that your donations are made in the most tax-efficient way so that you and your chosen charities get the most benefits. It also means weighing up your options from time to time, looking at how your chosen charities are performing – and whether there are other places you could give to as well. That's what this chapter aims to examine.

Should you choose to support international charities working in all sorts of needy areas – or should you look in your own community first? Is it better to give a little to a lot of different charities, or pick out a couple you think are important and give more to them?

Ask yourself what you really care about – what social problems or issues would you like to see alleviated? If you're concerned about poverty, say, do you want to send your money to help refugees in war-torn countries – or would you rather give to charities working with homeless people in your local area? Certain causes in the charity sector traditionally do very well in Britain, while others have to work a lot harder to raise money. Would you rather choose a charity which is slightly out of the public eye or do you want to support one with a lot of political clout?

Experts in the charity sector agree that no one should tell anyone which charities are right for them – giving is such a personal act that it's important that you make up your own mind. But there are a few questions you can ask yourself which may set you on the right track.

- Would I rather see a short-term relief of a particular problem – or a longer-term project to tackle its causes?
- How do I feel about charities which accept government funding, or work closely with government agencies? What about their links with big business?
- Do I want to give to a group which is concerned with advocacy and political aims – or would I rather give to a more hands-on charity?
- Do I want to see clear results coming from my own donation, or am I happy to be part of a wider effort?
- What kind of relationship do I want with a charity? Do I want lots of communication, newsletters and so on – or do I want to have a purely financial relationship?
- What other ways might I get involved? Do I want to take an active part in the work the organisation does?

What are the different ways I can give money?

First of all, there's one-off giving – the kind of thing you do when you call to pledge money to Red Nose Day or the Niger famine appeal or drop a pound coin in a collection box. Then there are regular or 'committed' giving schemes – they might be in the form of a membership (of a gallery or a nature reserve, say) or a sponsorship of some kind (a needy child, a clean water source in a village or even a zoo animal). This type of giving has the advantage of building up a relationship between a donor and their chosen charity. You feel like you're able to watch your money at work and participate to some extent in a charity's good work – and the charity gets a regular stream of income as well as the chance to approach you in future to give more or donate to a specific project. Everyone wins.

With so many charities wanting to tap into the committed-giver market, it's easy to see why groups of people with big smiles and clipboards have proliferated on British high streets. Face-to-face fundraisers – known by their detractors as 'charity muggers' or 'chuggers' for short – are a surprisingly effective force. The Public Fundraising Regulatory Association (PFRA) estimates that in 2004 face-to-face fundraising led to 690,000 people signing up for direct debit pledges. Of those, as many as three-quarters don't support any other charity. And it's estimated that each person who signs up will contribute an average of £350 over five years.[105]

The PFRA believes that if you don't ask, you don't get – and certainly it seems many people won't think about giving to charity until someone asks them. But most charities employ companies to do this face-to-face fundraising for them, and those companies do charge for their services. They're typically paid between £50 and £100 for each new sign-up. Now of course if you sign up to give in this way, you have every right to change your mind and cancel your direct debit. But the fees are paid to the fundraising company regardless, so if you cancel after just a couple of months, the charity will be out of pocket. If it happens often, the charity could be in serious trouble.[106]

In fact a number of British charities – Greenpeace among them – have decided to stop face-to-face fundraising. As the public becomes more and more irritated by chuggers, some organisations believe that it's actually hindering their fundraising efforts.[107] But for many others, it's still a very cost-effective way of signing up new donors and increasing public awareness about their work. Bear in mind, though, that the person trying to sign you up is obliged to tell you how much they're being paid to do so; and that if you sign up, you may have to keep donating for some time before the charity sees any benefit.

If you want to give to lots of different charities without the hassle of doing all the paperwork each time, one option could be a Charity Account run by the Charities Aid Foundation. You pay into the account through lump sums or regular giving and then pay out to any charity you like using 'charity cheques', online payments or direct debits. The Charity Account makes sure that all your giving is done tax-efficiently and provides an easy and flexible way to make donations.

Payroll giving is huge in the US – about a third of company employees give in this way, compared with a tiny 2 per cent of British employees.[108] But the British government is encouraging employers to put these schemes in place, and if you're paid through a pay-as-you-earn tax scheme then your employer is almost certainly eligible to offer payroll giving. If your workplace doesn't, why not suggest it? The government is currently offering cash incentives to small and medium-sized businesses and it will match employees' donations for the first six months. And if that's not enough to convince them, try casually mentioning that a third of companies who offer payroll giving believe it's helped them hang on to their staff.[109] It boosts morale and aids recruitment – not to mention enhancing the company's ethical profile.

How can I find out if a charity is legitimate?

First of all, look for the charity's registration number. If a charity is registered and has an annual income over £10,000 then it should mention that it's registered on all its documentation. Then you can check those details with the Charities Commission.

It's important to remember that registration doesn't necessarily mean that the Commission approves or endorses the charity's work. It just means the charity has gone through all the legal hoops to get registered. Many completely legitimate voluntary groups are not registered charities. That said, the fact that a charity has taken the trouble to do the paperwork says something about its level of commitment. It also means that you can find out all its details on the Charity Commission's website – see the Resources section in Chapter 6 for further information.

But even if an organisation isn't registered, if you're still interested in giving there are ways to check them out, too. For example, if they're a registered company you can search their details through the databases held at Companies House. It's worth asking the group for details about how it is set up and why it has decided to do it in this way – the answer could tell you all you need to know.[110]

Summer 2005 saw the launch of a new resource for potential donors – the GuideStar UK database. It's being launched in stages and when it's complete GuideStar UK will hold information about every registered charity in Britain. There will be full contact information, details about how the charity is structured and administered, a review of its activities and a whole host of financial information. Charities will also be able to supplement their database entries with additional information about their activities and accomplishments. The US-based Guidestar.org (which inspired GuideStar UK) has been running since 1994 and has amassed a huge mine of information about the non-profit sector. The UK site will allow charities to demonstrate their achievements – and it'll also help would-be donors find out more about where to give.

How can I find out what my money will be spent on?

If you ask to see a charity's most recent accounts, then that charity is legally obliged to provide them to you. Simple as that. This makes charities accountable not just to their members or donors, but also to the wider public. Under the Charities Act 1993 the charity can take up to two months to send the accounts to you – and they can also charge you for photocopying, postage and any other admin costs.

The Charity Commission also holds copies of all charities' accounts – as well as their governing documents and annual reports. There are plans to make this information available online, but currently if you want to approach the Commission to view accounts you'll have to contact them to make an appointment to look at their records – or pay a small fee to have a copy sent to you.

Once you get the accounts, though, it can be quite tricky to figure out what to look for. Yes, you can look at what proportion of the charity's funds are spent on administration costs or how much money the charity spends on fundraising activities. But as we've already discussed in Chapter 4, these don't always give the clearest picture. There may be reasons why your chosen charity seems to spend more on administration – and the fact that another organisation spends very little isn't always a good thing for its long-term prospects.

The charityfacts.org website suggests that it wouldn't want to support an organisation which spent less than 5 per cent of its total expenditure on good management – because it would wonder about its ability to achieve its goals if it was investing such a small amount on infrastructure. Likewise, it would have 'concerns' about charities which spent more than 15 per cent on admin – and would want to know why their expenses were so high.

Finally, accounts really can't give the whole picture of what a charity does. They tell part of the story, but it's also important to look at what the charity achieves. In order to do this, you have to dig a bit deeper.

How do I find out how effective a charity is?

Whether it's a fund to save a local church steeple or a huge international development organisation, a charity is effective if it's achieving its stated aims.

Get on the internet and start doing a bit of research. Most larger charities will have websites – dig around and see what you can find out. Also, try typing the charity's name into a search engine or a news site. How often do they come up in news stories? Does it seem from the coverage they've received that they have some leverage with important people?

For small, local charities information may be a bit harder to come by. The best thing to do is get out into your community and get nosy. Is the charity mentioned a lot in the local paper? What do people who live in your area think about the charity's work? Try asking at your local council offices, approach your church, mosque, synagogue or other place of worship, and check out the Citizens' Advice Bureau. There are also a few directories that might help: the National Federation of Community Organisations has a website at communitymatters.org.uk or you can contact your local Council for Voluntary Service.

Large or small, ask a charity for a copy of its annual report and governing documents – these should help you to get an idea about what the charity's general aims are. Any reputable charity should be happy to talk to you about the work it's doing and how successful its campaigns have been. What are they doing that's different, and what are their plans for the future?

GuideStar UK also gives charities the option to upload documents that detail their achievements and future plans.

How can I avoid becoming a victim of a scam?

As we saw in Chapter 4, there are a very few unscrupulous people out there who look to profit from other people's generosity – and while they're at it, they give the sector a bad name. Fortunately, there are a few easy things you can do to protect yourself against scammers and make sure that your money is going where it's needed most.

The Charity Commission is promoting a Safer Giving Code which sets out the things you should look for when giving money – and a few warning signs to heed.

Charity Commission Safer Giving Code

The Commission strongly recommends that all collectors should:

- be able to produce a valid local authority or police licence (note: a small minority of charities have a Home Office exemption order which allows them to collect without a licence)
- wear an ID badge (donors should look out for any ID that looks altered, photocopied or home-made)
- have a sealed collection container with the charity's registration number and name on it – does it match the details on their ID badge?
- be able to tell you how to contact the charity direct
- be able to prove that they have the charity's permission to collect.

Collectors from professional fundraising companies must, by law, declare how much of the donation they will be paid, and they should be able to produce a copy of a written agreement with the charity. Thank you letters and receipts from charities don't count!

If you are still doubtful about the collector:

- contact the Charity Commission to check the charity registration number or discuss any concerns – either via the helpline on 0870 333 0123 or by searching the online register at the Commission's website
- contact your local authority or police to check whether the collector has been granted a licence or needs one to collect
- above all, don't feel pressurised – send your donation to the charity direct. This may mean going to a little more trouble, but at least you can be sure that your donation will get to where it's intended.

There are a few other things to watch out for. Be wary of telemarketers who claim to be collecting for charity: if you're approached in this way, ask for a telephone number so that you can call the charity back and check them out. Don't be afraid to ask the charity to send you written information, and don't be pressurised into deciding to donate on the spot. Remember, a legitimate charity won't mind you doing any of these things.

On the internet, watch for bogus websites – some can be very convincing. Check out the name of the charity closely, as some scammers will try using a name that's very close to that of a well-known charity. Look for contact details on the website and take the time to call the charity in question. Be cautious about unsolicited 'spam' e-mails, chain letters and sites that have a lot of spelling and grammar errors. Remember, just as your bank would never e-mail you to ask to confirm your account details, a legitimate charity won't ask for sensitive financial information in an e-mail. If you have any doubts, telephone the charity direct to check.

If you're considering volunteering for any organisation – particularly one that will involve you travelling outside the UK – make sure you investigate it properly. Genuine charities will have websites and contact details. You should check to see if the group has links to well-known charities. Also consider contacting organisations working in the region to see if they know more about the scheme you're investigating.

And last of all, be smart about how you send your money. A cheque made out to the organisation is one safer way to give and giving by credit card offers you a greater measure of protection than a debit card.

If you have been approached by a fraudster or are worried about anyone who's approached you, you should contact the Charity Commission or your local police.

Once I've decided to give, what kind of protection do I have?

The Institute of Fundraising has developed a Donors' Charter which sets out a fundraiser's commitment to its donors. It sets out what donors can expect from charities and other fundraising bodies before, during and after their donation.

The Donors' Charter

When you consider making a gift to charity, we undertake that:
- all communications surrounding it will be honest and truthful, and will comply with the law
- your right to privacy will be respected and you will not be subjected to any form of pressure
- your gift will be applied to the purpose for which it was originally requested
- your gift will be used in a way that preserves the dignity of the beneficiary
- your gift will be handled responsibly and to the greatest advantage of the beneficiary
- fundraisers and the organisations that they represent will consider how they meet your wishes as a donor and will be transparent in their dealings with you
- fundraisers will respect your needs for confidentiality and will comply with the law relating to fundraising and the use of personal data
- fundraisers will strive to achieve the highest professional standards at all times.

Any concerns you may have relating to these points will be handled swiftly and effectively by the organisations with which they are raised.

The donors' charter also sets out complaints procedures and explains how the charity itself, the Institute of Fundraising and the Charity Commission are able to help.

There are a few other things that donors can expect from charities: a letter saying thank you for your donation and the option to receive more information about the charity and how your money is being used. They are obliged to abide by the rules of the Data Protection Act – which means that they must ask you if you are happy for them to share your personal details. Watch for tick boxes on application forms! If you say no, then they cannot pass your contact details on to anyone else. The charity should also be open and honest with you if you have any questions and it shouldn't put pressure on you to give more or get involved with other campaigns.[111]

A number of charities in Britain operate membership schemes, whereby a donor can take a more active role. The largest of these in the UK is the National Trust, which has some 3 million active members. Becoming a member of a charity may involve extra rights and responsibilities, like the right to vote at annual general meetings and the power to select trustees. All of these schemes operate slightly differently, so your charity should tell you what your membership entails and what you'll get in return.[112]

How can I get the most out of my donation?

Once you've chosen to give to a particular charity, make sure your donation is working as hard as possible by making it tax-effective. In Britain this means ensuring that you have donated through the Gift Aid scheme.

If you pay taxes in the UK, you can ask that the tax you've paid on your donation is given to the charity – and this means that for every £1 you give, the charity will get an extra 28 pence. So if you give £10 through Gift Aid, the charity gets £12.80. That's a pretty good deal, and it doesn't cost you any extra.

The problem is that a huge number of donations made in the UK are not done through the Gift Aid scheme. The Institute of Fundraising estimates that some £900 million in donations were not Gift Aided in 2004 – if they had been, charities would have received an extra £250 million.[113]

So if you want to maximise the amount of money your chosen charity will receive, check that your donation is Gift Aided – and if you want to go one step further, contact the charities you give to already to check whether those are done through Gift Aid too. If you haven't, then all is not lost – the Gift Aid contributions can be backdated to April 2000.

And if that's not enough, higher rate taxpayers can claim tax relief for donations they have made to charity – as much as £23 on a £100 donation.

There's also a scheme that offers tax relief to people who give shares to a charity. You might have shares that you've received as a result of a demutualisation, or perhaps you've inherited a number of small parcels of shares which are a nuisance to administer. You can even give land or buildings to charity and claim tax relief from that. If you've got that kind of money and you're interested in finding out more, the Inland Revenue's website has all the details.

Another way for your charity to get the most out of your money is to donate through a payroll giving scheme. If you choose this, donations will come out of your gross salary – before tax has been deducted. So if you want to give £10 to a charity, and you're paying basic rate tax, your donation will cost just £7.80.

I don't want to just give money. What else could I do?

There are some pretty inventive ways you can give to charity – it doesn't all have to be about direct debits and collection boxes.

One of the biggest hit gifts of Christmas 2004 was the humble goat. It's the ideal present for the person who has everything – Oxfam sold 30,000 of them and CAFOD another 13,000. Fans of the band Radiohead, who make it a tradition to buy the drummer Ed O'Brien strange Christmas gifts, bought dozens.[114] Your recipient gets a card telling them what you've bought for them, and a needy family gets a versatile animal that can be milked and bred from. Then the goat's first female baby is given to another family, enabling them to benefit from your gift, too.

Other **gift schemes** offer the chance to buy some truly unusual presents: Goodgifts.org offers, among many other things, a brain cell (just £15 buys you a sponsored brain cell and funds research into Alzheimer's, Parkinson's and other diseases), domestic appliances for needy families in the UK and a 'flying toilet' (a community latrine for a village in Africa). World Vision's GreatGifts.org offers high-rollers the chance to give a secondary school – a snip at just £3,300.

If you're considering a major celebration of some kind then many of these schemes give you the chance to create a gift list. Weddinglistgiving.com allows guests to make a donation to nominated charities on behalf of the happy couple, while GiveIt.co.uk offers a range of different lists where your friends can buy you condoms for the Terrence Higgins Trust, physiotherapy for amputees or personal alarms for the Suzy Lamplugh Trust.

Sponsoring children is another way of giving to charity that involves something more than just a gift of straight cash. A regular donation goes to help a child receive medical care, nutritious food and schooling – in return, children write letters and send photographs to their sponsors. Some charities like Action Aid also use a portion of the sponsorship money to fund community projects like wells or schools, and the children have a direct input into how the money is spent.

This is a controversial area, not least because it raises some of the issues we talked about in Chapter 4 – it does have overtones of the kind of patronising 'cold charity' of days gone by. The schemes are expensive to administer and children may become isolated from their communities. It's also argued that sponsorship doesn't address the causes of poverty.

That said, many people working in the international aid sector believe that sponsorship can be positive. It creates links between people who would never otherwise meet and there can be a real sense of connection between child and sponsor. It's also a form of giving that appeals to some people who would never otherwise give to this kind of charity.

Another form of giving that can be controversial is what's known as **cause-related marketing** – when an established consumer brand forges links with a charity and donates a portion of the price for goods or services. Business in the Community (BITC) highlights a few of its award winners: Yell's Yellow Woods challenge, which promotes recycling of Yellow Pages directories and has donated thousands to schools and the Woodland Trust; BT's fundraising and support for ChildLine; and coffee brand Percol's support for the Coffee Kids charity, to name just a few.[115] BITC's Cause Related Marketing Tracker estimates that in 2003, 82 partnerships raised more than £58.2 million for charities.[116]

On the face of it, this looks like a good deal all round – a good reputation for the brand, money for the charity, and consumers get to feel like they've supported a good cause with very little effort. But before you go out of your way to make a special purchase, take a quick look at the small print. Britain's Food Commission criticised the sweet manufacturer Cadbury's for a scheme where tokens from chocolate bars could be exchanged for sports equipment for schools. One set of posts and nets for volleyball would have required tokens from 5,440 bars of chocolate at a cost of £2,000 – and a total calorie count of some 1.25 million.[117] There's also no question that businesses benefit from the association with a charitable cause. But if you're purchasing a product that you were going to buy anyway, then it's great that some of the money can go to charity – even if it's only a few pennies.

Finally, another way of making your shopping a little less guilt-ridden is to investigate **affinity credit cards and charity banking**. Many of the major charities offer credit cards and they receive a donation when you sign up – then every time you use your card, they'll get a percentage of what you spend. Typically charities will get 25p for every £100 spent, which isn't a huge amount, and interest rates may be higher than with other cards. It's still something that's worth exploring.[118] Meanwhile, The Charity Bank offers savings accounts where your money will be invested in community-based projects and interest can be donated to charity, while Triodos Bank, a leading ethical bank, offers charity accounts where savings help to support charity lending.

What about volunteering?

There's something you can give which is just as valuable as money, perhaps more so: the gift of time. It's estimated that around 60 per cent of private giving is in the form of volunteering and this is worth £40 billion a year to the British economy. More than half of the population of Britain volunteer in some way, and a million more join in each year. And in 2005 – the Year of the Volunteer – both the government and the voluntary sector looked at ways to get even more people to give their time.

Why is the British public so keen on giving up its time – perhaps keener than giving money? It's probably something to do with the fact that we can actually see the difference our volunteer work makes – whereas with a charity, it can be harder to tell where your £10 donation has ended up. People volunteer because they want to 'give back', because they want to help build their community. They may do it because they're passionate about a particular cause or because they can see a clear need for their time and effort. Regardless of the motivation, it's clearly an important part of British society – and it's also crucial for the non-profit sector. Since nearly three-quarters of voluntary and community organisations employ no paid staff at all, it's volunteers that keep them on their feet and achieving their aims. And it's easy to see why the government sees this as such an important part of its drive to build citizenship and community involvement.

Volunteering can be done as part of a formal scheme, and 11 million Britons do this at least once a month. Common ways to help include organising activities or events, raising money, leading a group or being a member of a committee. The largest group of volunteers are involved in sports and leisure activities — helping to run clubs, refereeing matches at weekends. But there's a whole host of ways in which you can volunteer informally: giving advice, looking after property or pets for people while they're away, babysitting, giving someone a lift, doing their shopping.

Volunteering doesn't just make you feel good: a survey for ICM research found that nearly half of volunteers said their physical health and fitness had improved, while one in five said it had helped them lose weight. Among 18–24 year olds, nearly a quarter said that volunteering helped them cut down on alcohol, nearly a third said it helped them smoke less and 17 per cent said it improved their sex life.[119] Meanwhile, 81 per cent of employers surveyed by TimeBank viewed employees who do voluntary work positively, and nearly half said that employees who volunteer have a better chance of promotion and earning a better salary.[120]

So how do you get volunteering? There are a host of organisations that aim to match willing volunteers with their perfect post: TimeBank, Do-it and Volunteering England are just a few. More are listed in the Resources section in Chapter 6. There are a lot of weird and wonderful volunteering jobs you can do, too: you can be a toad warden (helping toads cross roads during breeding season), a tandem bike rider (taking partially sighted people out cycling) or a death row pen pal.[121]

If you already know where you'd like to volunteer, get in touch with the charity of your choice. Some larger charities have volunteer co-ordinators while others will deal with it through their personnel departments – still others will need you to make direct contact with the section you'd like to work in. The more you talk to your chosen organisation, the more you'll be able to work out what you can do for them – and what they can do for you. You can give as little as an hour a week, or you can make a long-term, full-time commitment – the options are endless, and every minute you can give will make a real difference.

And how about legacy giving – how important is that?

A legacy is an arrangement you make in your will to leave money to a charity after you die. These are a vital source of income to charities – in 2003–4 legacies were worth more than £1 billion. And yet they seem to be relatively unpopular: although nearly 70 per cent of Britons give to charity regularly, fewer than one in five leave money to charity in their will.[122] More worrying is the fact that one in five of us die without a will of any kind.

There are three different ways that you can give to charity in your will: a pecuniary legacy, where you give a fixed sum; a residual legacy, where you give a share of your whole estate; and a specific gift of property. All legacies to charity are free from inheritance tax, so what you give is what they receive.

Cancer relief is the sector which receives most money

from legacies; Cancer Research UK says that over half of its funding is in this form.[123] Other causes that do well are animal protection, environment and heritage charities, general social welfare and children's charities.

One of the most important things to bear in mind is that if you're going to leave money to charity in your will, you have to do it properly. The laws governing how estates are distributed are quite specific, and if changes aren't witnessed properly this can cause big problems.

So what should you do? First of all, it's a good idea to contact the charity you'd like to remember in your will and get their advice. They will be happy to help and many of them have information packs or specialist staff who can advise you about what to do. If you don't want to rewrite your whole will, your solicitor can help you prepare a codicil, which is a legally binding addition to an existing will. In addition to this, some solicitors may give discounts for this type of work – again, your chosen charity will be able to advise you further.

6

Resources

This chapter gathers together lots of information which will help you put into practice some of the ideas in this book. First we'll look at which are the most popular charity sectors, and the most popular ways of giving, then we'll profile Britain's biggest charities. Then there is a huge list of contacts which can help you to get in touch with charities, find out about fundraising and match up your skills to the right volunteering opportunity. It's not a completely exhaustive list, but it'll certainly help you get started. Finally, there's a glossary of terms used in the book to help you cut through the jargon.

Which are the most popular charity sectors?

As we mentioned in Chapter 1, when you look at overall income to each sector, international development consistently comes out on top, closely followed by cancer charities. The table overleaf gives a detailed breakdown of how the charity sectors stack up.

Voluntary income by charity sector

Sector	Voluntary income (£ millions)
International	654
Cancer	417
Religious – general services	356
Heritage/environmental	351
Arts/culture	341
Children	321
Religious missionary	290
Animal protection/rescue	257
General social welfare	241
Disability	181
Religious international	152
Chest and heart	124
Blind	120
Health advocacy/information/research	112
Hospices	105
Elderly	92
Hospitals	85
Services/ex-services	75
Youth	62
Mental health	56
Benevolent funds	54

Sector	Voluntary income (£ millions)
Israeli causes	50
Education	36
Deaf	33
Community development	30
Economic development	22
Recreation	18
Philanthropy and infrastructure	15
HIV/Aids	13

Source: Charities Aid Foundation 2005.

How do people give to charity?

Almost every person in the UK gives to charity at some point in any given year, and street and door-to-door collections remain the most popular method of giving. As you can see from the table below, although these methods may be common they generate just a small percentage of the total money given to charity each year. These 'low yield' methods of fundraising are still important, though, because this kind of collection plays a key part in promoting charities to a broader audience.

It's also interesting to note that some methods attract a higher yield – in other words, the amount raised as a proportion of the total given is greater than the proportion of people giving through those methods. These include giving through a subscription or membership scheme and sponsorship – methods which require a more active decision and a higher level of commitment from the donor.[124] This suggests that the more we think about our charity giving, the more we are happy to give!

Popularity and effectiveness of methods of giving

Method of giving	% of population	% of total given
Street collection	18.8	3.6
Door-to-door collection	15.5	4.0
Buying raffle/lottery tickets (not National Lottery)	12.2	4.7
Buying in a charity shop	10.6	8.0
Shop counter collection	10.2	1.9
Church collection	10.0	14.4
Sponsorship	9.0	12.6
Collection at work	6.0	2.4
Buying goods for a charity	5.5	4.2
Pub collection	4.9	1.0
Appeal letter	4.2	4.9
Buying in a jumble sale	4.1	2.0
Attending a charity event	4.3	6.0

Method of giving	% of population	% of total given
Subscription/membership fee	2.8	3.8
Covenant	2.5	8.7
Buying through a charity catalogue	1.4	2.1
TV or radio appeal	3.0	5.5
Payroll deduction	1.5	0.7
Telephone appeal	0.9	0.6
Appeal advertisement	0.8	1.7
Affinity card	0.1	0.1
Stocks and shares	0.2	0.1
Other gifts of money	4.8	7.2

Source: Charities Aid Foundation/NCVO, *Inside Research*, issue 21, October 2004.

What are the UK's ten largest charities, what do they do and how can I contact them?

As we saw in Chapter 1, the UK's top ten charities wield enormous financial power. These ten big hitters raised a quarter of all the income that went to the top 500 charities in the UK.

Income to the top ten charities in the UK

	Charity	Voluntary income (£ millions)
1	Cancer Research UK	306
2	The National Trust	144
3	Oxfam	134
4	British Heart Foundation (BHF)	119
5	Royal National Lifeboat Institution (RNLI)	91
6	Salvation Army	91
7	Macmillan Cancer Relief	84
8	NSPCC	82
9	RSPCA	76
10	Save the Children UK	70

Source: Charities Aid Foundation, 2003–4 figures.

Let's take a closer look at these ten super-charities.

1. Cancer Research UK

Cancer Research UK was created in February 2002 following the merger of Imperial Cancer Research Fund and the Cancer Research Campaign. This merged organisation is founded on a history of

www.cancerresearch uk.org
PO Box 123
Lincoln's Inn Fields
London WC2A 3PX
020 7242 0200

association between the two bodies dating back to 1902. Cancer Research UK describes itself as the world's largest independent organisation dedicated to cancer research, and the largest single funder of cancer research in the UK. The principal objectives of Cancer Research UK are to undertake leading-edge research into the biology and causes of cancer; to develop treatments and improve cancer patients' lives; to bring down the number of people who get cancer; and to provide high-quality information on cancer for the public and other relevant parties.

2. The National Trust

The National Trust was founded in 1895 by three Victorian philanthropists who were concerned about the consequences of industrialisation and unregulated development. The Trust was conceived as a body that would safeguard threatened coastline, countryside and buildings. More than a century later, the Trust cares for over 248,000 hectares (612,000 acres) of countryside in England, Wales and Northern Ireland, plus almost 600 miles of coastline and more than 200 buildings and gardens of outstanding interest and importance. In addition to these core works, the Trust helps educate people and shape debate about the importance of the environment and the role of heritage as a bridge between past, present and future.

www.nationaltrust.org.uk
London Central Office
36 Queen Anne's Gate
London
SW1H 9AS
0870 609 5380

3. Oxfam

As part of an effort to ensure that relief supplies reached civilians who were suffering from blockades during the Second World War, the Oxford Committee for Famine Relief met for the first time on 5 October 1942.

www.oxfam.org.uk
**Oxfam House
274 Banbury Road
Oxford
OX2 7DZ
0870 333 2700**

After the war was over the Oxford Committee continued its work and broadened its objectives. The Committee formally became Oxfam in 1965, a decade during which its focus shifted to the predicament of people in poorer countries. Oxfam describes its vision as 'a world where there is no longer poverty and suffering'. The organisation aims to help ensure that every individual is able to earn a reasonable and sustainable living, has access to education and health provision, has his or her life and security safeguarded in times of conflict and natural disaster, has a right to be heard by decision-makers, and has a right to a life free of gender or ethnic discrimination. Issues that Oxfam works on include trade, gender equality, education, HIV/Aids, debt and aid.

4. The British Heart Foundation

The British Heart Foundation (BHF) aims to play a leading role in battling heart disease. Founded in 1961, the organisation aims for a future where dis-

www.bhf.org.uk
**14 Fitzhardinge Street
London
W1H 6DH
020 7935 0185**

ease of the heart and circulation is no longer a principal cause of disability and premature death. The BHF counts itself as the largest independent funder of heart research in the UK. It funds approximately 1,200 research projects, investigating all dimensions of heart disease. As well as funding professors and nurses and the training of medical professionals, the BHF promotes education and public awareness. The organisation also provides life-saving cardiac equipment and supports patient rehabilitation and care.

5. Royal National Lifeboat Institution

In 1824, a lifeboatman called Sir William Hillary co-ordinated the first lifeboat service. His efforts led to the foundation of the National Institution for the Preservation of Life from Shipwreck, later to become the RNLI. One hundred years later, the RNLI had saved almost 60,000 lives and in 2004 the charity saved an average of 21 people each day. The RNLI provides the 24-hour lifeboat search and rescue service that operates for up to 50 miles out from the coast of the UK and Ireland. It also provides a beach lifeguard service on 57 beaches in the south-west of England. There are 232 lifeboat stations strategically placed around the UK and Ireland. In 1999 the RNLI marked 175 years of life-saving.

www.rnli.org.uk
West Quay Road
Poole
BH15 1HZ
0845 122 6999

6. The Salvation Army

The Salvation Army began life in London in the mid-18th century as 'The Christian Mission' – a movement founded by an ex-Methodist minister. In 1878, the Christian Mission rapidly expanded, both nationally and internationally, under its new name, the Salvation Army. Though the Salvation Army is primarily a Christian church with a doctrine informed by Christian beliefs, the Army assists all people regardless of faith. The Salvation Army describes itself as 'the largest provider of social care in the UK, after the Government'. Its work extends from child care to elderly care, from homelessness projects to addiction rehabilitation.

www2.salvationarmy.org.uk
Territorial Headquarters
101 Newington Causeway
London
SE1 6BN
0845 634 0101

7. Macmillan Cancer Relief

In 1911, Douglas Macmillan watched his father die of cancer. The pain and suffering his father went through moved Douglas to found the Society for the Prevention and Relief of Cancer, with the aim of promoting quality cancer care and information for everyone. Macmillan wanted to see 'homes for cancer patients throughout the

www.macmillan.org.uk
89 Albert Embankment
London
SE1 7UQ
0808 808 2020

land, where attention will be provided freely or at low cost, as circumstances dictate'. The charity began building hospices in 1969 and changed its name to Macmillan Cancer Relief in 1997. Today Macmillan supports people with cancer through every stage of their journey – in contrast with Cancer Relief UK, which concentrates on scientific research and treatment.

8. NSPCC

The NSPCC (National Society for the Prevention of Cruelty to Children) describes itself as the UK's leading charity specialising in child protection and the prevention of cruelty to children. The NSPCC was founded in 1884 as the London SPCC in an effort to prompt government and public action in relation to largely unrecognised problems of cruelty to children. The organisation works to end cruelty to children and towards a society free from child abuse of any kind. In practical terms, the NSPCC's activities include running a child protection helpline, carrying out public education initiatives and parliamentary campaigning, conducting research into the nature and effects of child abuse and providing child protection training and advice. The organisation is the only UK children's charity with statutory powers that enable it to take action to safeguard children at risk of abuse. The NSPCC has helped over 10 million children since it began its work in the 1880s.

www.nspcc.org.uk
Weston House
42 Curtain Road
London
EC2A 3NH
020 7825 2500

9. The RSPCA

The Royal Society for the Prevention of Cruelty to Animals (RSPCA) has a vision of a world in which all humans respect and live in harmony with the animal kingdom. The organisation works to relieve animal suffering and enforce the law by providing animal welfare services, by educating people and by campaigning for better treatment for animals, including through better legislation. Much of the RSPCA's operational activities concern animal treatment and re-homing as well as investigation into complaints of animal cruelty. The Society became the first organisation of its kind in the world when it was founded as the SPCA in London in 1824. By permission of Queen Victoria, the Society incorporated 'Royal' into its name in 1840. From its initial work in London the RSPCA expanded to form a national network of 177 branches in England and Wales. In 2003, RSPCA inspectors investigated 105,932 animal cruelty complaints which resulted in 1,829 convictions.

www.rspca.org.uk
Wilberforce Way
Southwater
Horsham
West Sussex
RH13 9RS
0870 33 35 999

10. Save the Children UK

Originally named The Fight the Famine Council, Save the Children was founded as a response to conditions in Europe immediately following the First World

www.savethechildren.org.uk
1 St John's Lane
London
EC1M 4AR
020 7012 6400

War. The Save the Children Fund was publicly launched in London in 1919 and started to raise money to send to European children living in war-devastated areas. Intended as a temporary organisation, Save the Children found that successive emergencies called for a more permanent existence. The work of Save the Children is built on a commitment to realising children's rights as enshrined in the UN Convention on the Rights of the Child. The organisation describes its vision as a world in which children have hope and opportunity and where they can reach their full potential. Save the Children works in the UK and across the world providing emergency relief as well as carrying out longer-term development and prevention initiatives.

Which are the ten biggest international development charities in the UK and what do they do?

As we saw above, international charities consistently raise the most voluntary income out of all the UK charities (by voluntary income, we mean donations, grants, legacies, charity shop income and Lottery grants). The table overleaf shows the ten biggest players in this sector.

Income to the top ten international development charities in the UK

Charity	Voluntary income (£ millions)
1 Oxfam	134
2 Save the Children UK	70
3 British Red Cross Society	67
4 Action Aid	52
5 Concern Worldwide	47
6 World Emergency Relief	30
7 World Vision UK	29
8 Plan International (UK)	26
9 Sight Savers International	24
10 UNICEF-UK	20

Source: Charities Aid Foundation, 2003–4 figures. Note that the CAF definition of international excludes the religious international and Israeli charities as they are placed in separate categories.

Oxfam and Save the Children UK are profiled above – here are some details about the rest of the top ten.

3. The British Red Cross

The British Red Cross is a part of the largest independent humanitarian organisation in the world – the International Red Cross and Red Crescent Movement. Inspired by the wartime suffering in the mid-19th century, the International Red Cross and Red Crescent movement grew out of a perceived need for neutral and impartial assistance to relieve the human damage of conflict. The founder of the Red Cross movement, Henry Dunant, was also behind the original Geneva Convention – an international agreement that countries recognise the status of medical services and of the wounded on the battlefield. Following on from examples set in other countries, the British National Society for Aid to the Sick and Wounded in War was formed in 1870. In 1905 this society became the British Red Cross Society and was granted its first Royal Charter. The core of the British Red Cross's work concerns the provision of relief for people in crisis – both in the UK and overseas. Besides its role in training first aiders, the Red Cross supplies food, water, shelter and medicines in response to conflicts and disasters.

www.redcross.org.uk
UK Office
44 Moorfields
London
EC2Y 9AL
0870 170 7000

4. Action Aid

Action Aid began in 1972 by launching sponsorship programmes for children in India and Kenya. Since then the organisation has broadened its scope to working on root causes of poverty and marginalisation.

www.actionaid.org
Hamlyn House
Macdonald Road
London
N19 5PG
020 7561 7561

While Action Aid helps people secure access to, for example, food, water and healthcare, these basics are approached as part of a broader project to help poor people to organise themselves and to claim their rights. Action Aid's vision is of a world without poverty in which every person can exercise his or her right to a life of dignity. The organisation's mission is 'to work with poor and marginalised people to eradicate poverty by overcoming the injustice and inequity that cause it'. Action Aid campaigns on issues such as food rights, education and HIV/Aids.

5. Concern Worldwide

Concern grew out of alarm at the suffering caused by the 1968 famine in Biafra, Nigeria. A group of individuals in Ireland established Africa Concern. The group raised money to send ships with

www.concern.net
52–55 Lower Camden Street
Dublin 2
Republic of Ireland
(+353) 1 417 7700

relief supplies to west Africa. Following further relief activity for victims of a cyclone in Pakistan in 1970, Africa Concern became Concern. Its stated mission is to enable poor people to achieve major and sustainable improvements in their lifestyles. This is part of a vision to create just and peaceful societies where the poor can exercise their fundamental rights. Concern carries out long-term development work, responds to emergency situations, and undertakes development education and advocacy on poverty issues. The organisation's headquarters are in Dublin.

6. World Emergency Relief

World Emergency Relief (WER) was first founded in America in the 1980s by Reverend Joel MacCollam to address the needs of children across the world. The UK branch was established in 1995.

www.wer-uk.org
20 York Buildings
London
WC2N 6JU
0870 429 2129

WER describes itself as 'a non-denominational, global fellowship of Christians, working together and with others to help children in need'. There are now branches of WER in Germany, Holland and Hong Kong. The organisation works with local partners in 25 countries and has a strong Gifts In Kind programme, where individuals and businesses can donate goods (like seeds, clothing, baby food, even a fire engine!) which will be sent directly to needy countries.

7. World Vision UK

World Vision is a Christian charity that helps people of all religions who are battling against poverty, hunger and injustice. An American missionary founded World Vision following a trip to China and Korea in 1947 during which he became convinced of the need to send money directly in order to address poverty and a lack of basic provisions. In 1950, World Vision was legally incorporated as an organisation and offices were established in numerous countries. World Vision UK was registered as a charity in 1982. World Vision describes the basis of its response to human need as deriving from its 'holistic understanding of the Kingdom of God'. The organisation's work relates to emergencies as well as to longer-term development initiatives. In addition to running child sponsorship programmes, World Vision concentrates on issues such as HIV/Aids, peace and conflict and children's rights.

www.worldvision.org.uk
Opal Drive
Fox Milne
Milton Keynes
MK15 0ZR
01908 841000

8. Plan International (UK)

In 1937 British journalist John Langdon-Davies and refugee worker Eric Muggeridge were so moved by the plight of refugees and orphans of the Spanish Civil

www.plan-uk.org
5–6 Underhill Street
London
NW1 7HS
020 7482 9777

War that they decided to set up the Foster Parents Plan for Children in Spain. When the Second World War began the organisation widened its scope to other European countries – eventually becoming involved in helping children in 45 countries across Asia, Africa and South America. Its name changed to Plan International in the 1990s and its UK branch is one of sixteen national organisations. Plan UK receives most of its income from child sponsorship programmes – more than 116,000 people sponsor a child through them.

9. Sight Savers International

Sight Savers International is dedicated to combating blindness in developing countries, primarily the Commonwealth. It says its vision is of a world where no one is needlessly blind and where everyone who is irreversibly blind or sight-impaired enjoys the same rights, responsibilities and opportunities as sighted people. It was established in the early 1950s by Sir John Wilson and in 2004 the organisation (along with its local partners) treated more than 3 million people for sight-related problems and protected 11 million people from river blindness.

www.sightsavers.org.uk
Grosvenor Hall
Bolnore Road
Haywards Heath
West Sussex
RH16 4BX
01444 446 600

10. UNICEF-UK

UNICEF-UK is one of 37 National Committees that raise funds for UNICEF, the United Nations International Children's Emergency Fund. UNICEF was established by the UN in 1946 to address the needs of children in Europe and China in the wake of the Second World War, and its remit was widened to include all developing countries in 1950. UNICEF works with local communities and governments in 157 countries to provide emergency relief and run long-term development programmes in areas like health, education and child protection. In addition to fundraising, UNICEF-UK works within the UK to raise awareness of issues affecting children around the world and lobby government to support children's rights. It also carries out one child health programme within the UK: the Baby Friendly Initiative which works with parents and health professionals to encourage breast-feeding.

www.unicef.org.uk
Africa House
64–78 Kingsway
London
WC2B 6NB
0870 606 3377

What about international appeals for disasters? What is the Disasters Emergency Committee?

The appeal to help the victims of the tsunami in South-East Asia saw the Disasters Emergency Committee (DEC) – an

www.dec.org.uk
15 Warren Mews
London
W1T 6AZ
020 7387 0200

umbrella group of UK international aid agencies – come into the public eye like never before. DEC launched and co-ordinated the UK's national appeal and it raised a record-breaking £400 million for the tsunami victims.

But what you might not know is that DEC was created more than 40 years ago, in 1963. DEC currently has thirteen member agencies: Action Aid, the British Red Cross, CAFOD, CARE International, Christian Aid, Concern, Help the Aged, Islamic Relief, Merlin, Oxfam, Save the Children, Tearfund and World Vision.[125]

DEC sets out its objectives as follows: 'creating an efficient appeal mechanism through the media for national fundraising and public response, ensuring that funds raised are used in an effective, timely and fully accountable way, facilitating agency co-operation, co-ordination and communication [and] raising standards in the implementation of humanitarian responses'.

DEC will launch an appeal where there is a major disaster or emergency which cannot be dealt with by that country's usual infrastructure and where DEC member agencies can respond quickly and effectively.

What crises has DEC responded to, and what has it achieved?

Here are a few selected examples of recent crises where DEC has launched appeals – and some independent evaluations of where the British public's money went.

Mozambique Floods Appeal
Launched on: 2 March 2000
Amount raised: £30 million

Severe flooding in Mozambique in the first quarter of 2000 devastated rural and urban communities. Some 700 people died and the floods destroyed houses, crops, livestock and livelihoods – they were described as the worst in living memory. DEC agencies moved families to safe places and provided food, water and shelter to families in temporary accommodation. They 'provided timely assistance that was largely appropriate to needs and to the local context and that had a real impact on the lives of those affected by the floods.'[126]

India Earthquake Appeal
Launched on: 1 February 2001
Amount raised: £24 million

On 26 January 2001 India suffered its most severe earthquake for half a century. The north-western state of Gujarat was worst affected. More than 16,000 people died and nearly a million lost their homes. In the worst-affected areas 95 per cent of buildings were destroyed. DEC was found to have given 'substantial and timely assistance', but its members could have developed more effective partnerships with local agencies.[127]

Goma Crisis Appeal
Launched on: 24 January 2002
Amount raised: £4.65 million

In January 2002, some 400,000 inhabitants of Goma in the Democratic Republic of Congo fled their homes after the Nyiragongo volcano erupted. Evaluators found that even though there had been warnings that a volcanic eruption was imminent, DEC members (and others) did not have a well-prepared and rehearsed plan for evacuation and rescue. But they judged that the DEC members who were present at the time of the disaster 'responded immediately and in an appropriate way'.[128]

Southern Africa Crisis Appeal
Launched on: 25 July 2002
Amount raised: £16 million

The Southern Africa Crisis Appeal was the first time that DEC held an appeal to prevent a humanitarian crisis rather than respond to one that had already happened. After two years of drought, flooding in some areas and political instability, more than 14 million people in seven southern African countries were facing starvation, and DEC wanted to fund a major food aid operation to avert a looming catastrophe.

It was found that DEC's agencies didn't always have a deep enough understanding about the communities where they were working, and 'the chronic roots of the crisis were understated'. The evaluation concluded that the appeal was justified – but that there was much to be learnt from it.[129]

Liberia Crisis Appeal
Launched on: 12 August 2003
Amount raised: £2.5 million

DEC launched the Liberia appeal to respond to the survival needs of some 600,000 Liberians displaced by a long and bloody civil war. An independent evaluation concluded that 'overall, the DEC projects ... were impressive and met essential needs' despite 'considerable challenges'.[130]

Where can I go to find out more information about charities, fundraising, volunteering and so on?

There are many, many groups out there that can help you find out more about all kinds of giving. This list gives details of the main regulators and industry organisations, plus a selection of other directories and websites that can help you get in touch with charities and find out more about fundraising and volunteering opportunities. It's not exhaustive, but we hope it will point you in the right direction!

Before you get in touch, though, it's worth thinking through a few of the issues we've discussed in the book. What kind of charity do you want to give to – large or small, local or national or even international, one that tackles root causes of problems or one that helps pick up the pieces?

And what kind of relationship do you want – do you just want to give money and let them get on with it, or would you like to investigate getting more involved with what the charity does?

If you're interested in volunteering, have a think about the kind of work you'd like to do. Are you looking for a one-off opportunity or a more regular commitment? If you fancy volunteering on a regular basis, how much time can you give and how often? Do you have any particular skills which would be useful, and are there any skills you'd like to learn?

There are many, many charities and other not-for-profit groups out there and all of them will be happy to receive your donation of time or money. But by asking yourself a few questions and figuring out what's important, you'll find the search for your ideal charity a lot easier.

Charity regulators

The Charity Commission
www.charity-commission.gov.uk
0870 333 0123

The Charity Commission is the regulator and registrar of charities in England and Wales. Its stated aim is 'to increase charities' efficiency and effectiveness and public confidence and trust in them'.

Most charities in England and Wales have to register with the Commission. The Register of Charities is available on the Commission's website or you can visit any of their offices – London, Taunton, Liverpool and Newport. Charities with incomes over £10,000 a year must send their accounts and annual report to the Commission each year and these are also publicly available.

The Commission provides advice and guidance to 24,000 charities each year. It also issues a wide range of publications aimed at both the public and people working within the sector. The Commission has strong powers to investigate and deal with fraud or dishonesty within charities and the results of inquiries held by the Commission are also published on the website.

The Office of the Scottish Charity Regulator (OSCR)
www.oscr.org.uk
01382 220 446

The Office of the Scottish Charity Regulator (OSCR) is the regulator for Scottish charities. Its vision is 'a flourishing charities sector in which the public has confidence, underpinned by OSCR's effective delivery of its regulatory role'.

The OSCR is a relatively new body and eventually it will perform similar functions to the Charity Commission. It is currently developing a regulatory framework under which all charities in Scotland will be monitored; from 2005 all charities regardless of size had to complete an Annual Return and from April 2006 they will have to submit accounts as well. Those with annual incomes over £25,000 have additional reporting requirements. The OSCR's 'The

List' programme will provide an online database of all 24,000 charities in Scotland.

Northern Ireland – Department for Social Development
www.dsdni.gov.uk
028 90 829 414

Northern Ireland has no formal system of registration for charities – all that charities need to do is register with the Inland Revenue for charitable status for tax purposes. The Department for Social Development is the charity administrator for Northern Ireland. Its main functions are giving consent to trustees to dispose of land or buildings held by charities and making schemes to change the objects of charities. It also gives informal advice to trustees and their solicitors.

Information about charities

Charities Aid Foundation
www.cafonline.org
01732 520000

CAF (Charities Aid Foundation) is an international NGO providing specialist financial services to charities and their supporters. It regards its purpose as 'to do all in its power to ensure that charitable giving to all charities is as robust and effective as it can possibly be'. It also encourages debates about the role of the non-profit sector and conducts research and advocacy.

CAF has a number of established websites that serve the charitable sector:

- CAF Online (www.cafonline.org) – an online guide to the products and multi-disciplinary services it offers to charities, individuals and companies across the globe.
- All About Giving (www.allaboutgiving.org) – a one-stop guide to tax-effective giving with lots of information about giving one-off gifts, payroll giving and getting the maximum tax benefit from your charity donations.
- CCInet (www.ccinet.org) – the Corporate Community Investment site aims to help companies achieve the greatest impact from their community programmes.
- CharityNet (www.charitynet.org) – a database of information, listings and links to the sites and activities of NGOs around the world.
- GiveNow (www.givenow.org) – online giving and fundraising destination, founded by CAF and the AOL Time Warner Foundation.

The Citizenship Foundation
www.citizenshipfoundation.org.uk

The Citizenship Foundation aims to empower individuals to engage in the wider community through education about the law, democracy and society. It focuses particularly on developing young people's citizenship skills, knowledge and understanding. It has adopted the 'Giving Nation' youth charity programme which aims to get young people involved in fundraising and giving.

The National Council for Voluntary Organisations (NCVO)

www.ncvo-vol.org.uk

0800 2 798 798

The National Council for Voluntary Organisations (NCVO) is the umbrella body for the voluntary sector in England. NCVO represents the views of the voluntary sector to policy makers and government and carries out in-depth research to promote a better understanding of the sector and its activities.

Services offered by NCVO include a freephone help desk, which anyone involved in the sector can call for expert advice, as well as policy briefings, information networks, events and a wide range of publications.

Databases, listings and factsheets about charities

GuideStar UK

www.guidestar.org.uk

GuideStar UK is an independent charity established in 2003 with the aim of promoting and supporting the UK's voluntary and community sector. Guidestar UK's website offers a free, comprehensive and easily accessible source of information about charities' activities and finances.

The first phase of Guidestar UK's activities came online in summer 2005 and covers the 167,000 registered charities in England and Wales. Phase Two will include Scotland and Northern Ireland, as well as 'excepted' and 'exempt' charities in England and Wales. Guidestar UK not only includes charity reports and accounts, but will give charities the opportunity to supplement their online entries with information about their future plans, successes and current work.

Charity Choice
www.charitychoice.co.uk

Charity Choice is another source of information – publishing separate editions of its annual reference book for the UK, Scotland and Northern Ireland as well as the Charity Choice Services Directory. The books include contact details and charity descriptions. The Charity Choice website includes an online database and resources to help donors explore giving options. There's also a Goodwill Gallery which allows people to give goods, time or skills to their chosen charity.

Charities Direct
www.charitiesdirect.com

CharitiesDirect.com is another searchable online charity database which provides information on over 10,000 UK charities. The site can help you find charities or groups of charities and allows you to check income and expenditure of the top 500 charities.

Charity Portal
www.charityportal.org.uk

Charity Portal is yet another database – this one lets users find charities by overall purpose and get their contact details, registration details and website addresses. There is a secure Click-to-Donate facility which allows you to give to your chosen charity immediately! You can also vote for your favourite charity.

New Philanthropy Capital
www.philanthropycapital.org

New Philanthropy Capital (NPC) is a registered charity that seeks to develop and encourage more effective philanthropy. The group works with donors and the voluntary sector and produces the Voluntary Agencies Directory, which lists over 2,000 national charities and other organisations connected to the voluntary sector. The Directory sets out each charity's contact details, aims and objectives. The NPC also carries out research and analysis to work out how and where funds and resources can be targeted most effectively.

Charity Facts
www.charityfacts.org

Charity Facts is a website which gives impartial information about how to give to charity and what to look for in the organisations you support. It includes advice about fundraising and administration costs. It is run by Professor Adrian Sargeant of Bristol Business School and is endorsed by the Institute of Fundraising.

Remember a Charity
www.rememberacharity.org.uk

The Remember a Charity website explains how to help a charity by including it in your will. It was launched by a group of more than 130 charities and is backed by a wide variety of legal and financial professional bodies – it includes lists of things to remember when making a will and can put you in touch with solicitors throughout the UK who can help.

Fundraising

Institute of Fundraising
www.institute-of-fundraising.org.uk
020 7840 1000

The Institute of Fundraising is the professional body which represents fundraisers – seeking to 'promote the profession of fundraising at every applicable level and opportunity'. It is the author of the Donors' Charter and its website contains some links and information about giving to charity and volunteering.

Public Fundraising Regulatory Association
www.pfra.org.uk
020 7401 8452

The Public Fundraising Regulatory Association (PFRA) is a voluntary self-regulatory body for fundraising organisations – it covers fundraisers who invite you to sign up by direct debit on the street and door-to-door. The PFRA promotes a code of conduct and allocates sites for fundraising. Its website contains details of how to complain if you think fundraisers are in breach of the code of practice.

Charity Check
www.charitycheck.org.uk

Charity Check provides a service mainly to local authorities and owners of retail premises, enabling them to check that any charity collection they authorise is genuine – that the charities are reputable and that collectors are authorised.

Charity Check also runs a website called Charity Collections (www.charitycollections.org) which provides information about which fundraising collections are in order – and which aren't.

Charities Trust
www.charitiestrust.org

The Charities Trust is a national payroll giving and corporate donation management agency approved by the Inland Revenue. Through its website you can make secure online donations to charities and open your own charity account or fundraising account.

Justgiving
www.justgiving.com

Justgiving is an online fundraising site which allows individuals to build their own fundraising page – if you're participating in a sponsored event, it allows you to upload photographs, send thank you messages and keep an eye on progress towards your target. It also enables your supporters to give quickly and tax-efficiently.

Information about volunteering

Volunteering England
www.volunteering.org.uk
0845 305 6979

Volunteering England works to promote volunteering as a powerful force for change, both for those who volunteer and for the wider community.

If you want to volunteer, its website can direct you towards volunteer centres or help you find opportunities overseas; it can also provide lots of ideas for those who'd like to give their time but are not sure what they want to do. It also offers resources for those who work with volunteers and is committed to developing an infrastructure to promote volunteering at all levels.

Volunteering England also maintains the Employee Volunteering website (www.employeevolunteering.org.uk) to help businesses organise volunteer work for their employees.

Wales Council for Voluntary Action
www.wcva.org.uk
0870 607 1666

WCVA is the voice of the voluntary sector in Wales, representing and campaigning for voluntary organisations, volunteers and communities in Wales. Its website includes information for anyone with an interest in volunteering.

Once you've decided to give your time, check out www.volunteering-wales.net, which matches up willing people with opportunities – as well as a whole host of useful resources.

Volunteer Development Scotland
www.vds.org.uk
01786 479593

Volunteer Development Scotland promotes, supports and develops volunteering in Scotland. For information about how to find volunteering opportunities near you, visit www.volunteerscotland.info (the website of the Volunteer Centre Network Scotland) or www.workwithus.org.

The Volunteer Development Agency (Northern Ireland)
www.volunteering-ni.org
028 9023 6100

The Volunteer Development Agency provides support, training and information on volunteering – including fact sheets about what's involved in volunteering and how to find organisations that need your help.

REACH
www.volwork.org.uk

REACH matches the skills of managers, professionals, businesspeople and technical experts with organisations that need their help across the UK. It claims to support a cross-section of the UK voluntary sector, from large national charities to small grass-roots community groups.

Community Service Volunteers
www.csv.org.uk

CSV aims to reconnect people to their community through volunteering and training, and its website offers a huge range of specialist programmes, including senior and youth volunteering and weekend volunteering projects in London.

Do-it
www.do-it.org.uk

Do-it's website provides a national database of volunteering opportunities, the majority of which come from local Volunteer Centres in England. The website also offers lots of information about volunteering, including overseas and residential opportunities.

Professionals4free
www.professionals4free.org.uk

Professionals4free is a website designed to link voluntary

and community groups looking for free professional help with professionals who want to volunteer. It also provides links to brokers of free (or subsidised) professional services.

Volunteers' Week
www.volunteersweek.org.uk

Volunteers' Week (1–7 June) is the UK's annual celebration of volunteering during which events are held across the country to recognise, reward and recruit volunteers. The site provides information on the week and its events.

TimeBank
www.timebank.org.uk

TimeBank encourages people to 'give time'. The site offers several different channels for access to volunteering opportunities – including a section on 'virtual volunteering', which allows you to use your computer skills to mentor young people or help community groups.

Experience Corps
www.experiencecorps.co.uk

The Experience Corps is an independent company set up to encourage people aged 50 and over to offer their skills and experience in their local communities. The site includes a section for 'armchair action' – types of volunteering that older people can do while they're going about their daily lives.

National Association of Citizens' Advice Bureaux
www.citizensadvice.org.uk

The UK network of Citizens' Advice Bureaux (CABs) helps people resolve legal, financial and social problems with free confidential advice. The CAB says there's a high demand for volunteer advisers!

Millennium Volunteers
www.millenniumvolunteers.gov.uk

Designed for 16–24 year olds, Millennium Volunteers is a scheme to help young people give time to their local communities. The site helps match volunteering opportunities with the interests and post codes of prospective volunteers.

Voluntary Service Overseas (VSO)
www.vso.org.uk

VSO is an international development charity that works through volunteers. It provides volunteer placements (usually for two years) in Africa and Asia for skilled and qualified individuals. Positions are available for a wide variety of skills, from performing arts to IT and accounting.

Student Volunteering England
www.studentvolunteering.org.uk

Student Volunteering England promotes student volunteering from one-off events to full-time gap year programmes.

In addition to co-ordinating Student Volunteering Week it works to provide students with volunteering opportunities and effective support.

National Association of Councils for Voluntary Service (NACVS)
www.nacvs.org.uk
and
Scottish Council for Voluntary Organisations (SCVO)
www.scvo.org.uk

Across the UK, Councils for Voluntary Service (CVS) are set up and run by local groups to promote local voluntary and community action. NACVS acts as umbrella body for CVSs across England, while the SCVO does the same in Scotland. Among other things, the sites show you how to contact your local CVS and give links to regional networks.

Glossary of terms and abbreviations

CAF – Charities Aid Foundation, an international NGO which provides specialist financial services to charities and their supporters. It also conducts a large body of research and forms policy on the non-profit sector.

Charity – an organisation that is recognised as charitable by the Charity Commission (in England and Wales), the Office of the Scottish Charity Regulator or the Inland Revenue (in Northern Ireland). A charity needs to have a purpose that is recognised as charitable, and needs to be for the benefit of the public.

Charity Commission – the registrar and regulator of charities in England and Wales. The Office of the Scottish Charity Regulator performs the same function in Scotland. There is no requirement for charities to register in Northern Ireland – charities there are administered by the Department for Social Development.

Charitable purpose – in order to register as a charity, an organisation must have a purpose that is charitable. The new Charities Bill introduces a list of twelve charitable purposes and these are set out in Chapter 2, pages 44–5.

Chugger – a slang term, from the phrase 'charity mugger', which refers to people who conduct face-to-face fundraising on the street.

Gross domestic product (GDP) – refers to the total value of all goods and services produced in a particular country within a specified period, usually a year. Since it gives a picture of the size of a given country's economy, it is useful for measuring the relative size of that country's donations to charity.

Legacy – a gift to a particular charity specified in a person's will.

NGO – stands for non-governmental organisation and usually refers to any not-for-profit group which is not set up by a government or state. It generally refers to social, economic, political or environmental advocacy groups – some of these will be charities too.

NCVO – the National Council for Voluntary Organisations, which is the umbrella group for the voluntary sector in England. The NCVO represents the views of the sector to governments and carries out in-depth research.

Non-profit/not-for-profit – an organisation which doesn't seek to generate a profit but works to achieve a given social outcome. 'The non-profit sector' is often used as a term to cover all voluntary organisations, whether they are charities or not.

Public benefit – in order to obtain charity status, groups must prove that they not only have a charitable purpose, but also operate for the benefit of the public. This is explained in more depth in Chapter 2 (pages 36–7).

Tax-efficient giving – refers to a method of donating to charity which takes full advantage of the various tax incentives offered by governments. One way of giving tax-efficiently is to ensure that you're giving through the Gift Aid scheme, which means that if you're a UK taxpayer and you donate to charity, the Inland Revenue will give the charity the portion of tax you have paid on your donation (usually 28 per cent). There are more details on tax-efficient giving in Chapter 5, pages 98–100.

UN – the United Nations, an international organisation formed in 1945 and made up of 191 states. It has a number of humanitarian and human rights arms which sometimes work in conjunction with other NGOs.

Volunteer – a person who gives their time to help another person outside their home or an organisation without payment. Volunteering can take many forms, including one-off events, regular commitments or informal arrangements.

Get online and get talking

Jessica Williams will be donating all royalties due to her from sales of this book (and Icon Books will contribute the same amount again) to a fund to be donated to charity.

You can help decide to which charity – or charities – this money will be given by voicing your opinions on the book's website:

www.howtogivetocharity.org

There's plenty more to read on the site too and we want your input so ... get involved.

Notes

1 'Giving to the Tsunami Disaster Appeal', Charities Aid Foundation Research and Policy Briefing, March 2005.
2 www.dec.org.uk/index.cfm/asset_id,873/index.html.
3 'Charity Sets Off Storm with Tsunami Aid Halt', *International Herald Tribune*, 7 January 2005.
4 Charities Aid Foundation Research and Policy Briefing, op. cit.
5 ICM poll for the National Council of Voluntary Organisations, February 2005, available at www.icmresearch.co.uk/reviews/2005/NCVO%20Charity%20Opinion%20Poll%20Feb%2005/NCVO%20Charity%20Poll%20-%20Feb05.asp.
6 'Charities Suffer as Britons Run Short after Tsunami Plea', *The Times*, 15 February 2005.
7 Charities Aid Foundation Research and Policy Briefing, op. cit.
8 Devinda R. Subasinghe, Sri Lanka's ambassador to the United States and Mexico, quoted in www.nonprofitresearch.org/usr_doc/MAYSnapShotspdf.pdf.
9 Charities Aid Foundation, October 2004, www.cafonline.org/news/news_story.cfm?whichStory=3324.
10 ICM Research poll for NCVO, accessed at www.icmresearch.co.uk/reviews/2003/ncvo-poll-feb-03.htm.
11 www.learningtogive.org.
12 Norman Alvey, *From Chantry to Oxfam: A Short History of Charity and Charity Legislation*, British Association for Local History, 1995.
13 Ibid.
14 Survey conducted by the Charity Commission, December 2001, reported at www.volresource.org.uk/kcnews/news508.htm.
15 Quoted in Lynn Abrams, 'Ideals of Womanhood: Cookery

Books as a Primary Source', BBC History, www.bbc.co.uk/history/lj/victorian_britainlj/source_idealwom_01.shtml.
16 Gustave Dore and Blanchard Jerrold, *London: A Pilgrimage*, 1872, chapter 21, reprinted at www.victorianlondon.org.
17 Andrew Carnegie, 'The Gospel of Wealth', 1889.
18 'Opening Up to Charity', *Time*, Europe edition, 13 September 2004.
19 'Doing Well and Doing Good', *Economist*, 31 July 2004.
20 'Fears of the Leviathan', *Guardian*, 9 March 2005.
21 Charities Aid Foundation, www.cafonline.org/research/default.cfm.
22 Charities Aid Foundation/National Council for Voluntary Organisations, 'Charitable Giving in 2003', *Inside Research*, issue 21, October 2004.
23 Ibid.
24 Ibid. Classifications of the A, B, C1, C2, D and E classes come from the National Readership Survey, www.nrs.co.uk.
25 Family Expenditure Survey, quoted in C. Pharoah and S. Tanner, 'Trends in Charitable Giving', *Fiscal Studies* (1997), vol. 18, no. 4, pp. 427–43.
26 Adrian Sargeant, 'What Turns Donors On? What Turns Them Off?', *A Lot Of Give*, Charities Aid Foundation, 2002, p. 172.
27 Survey from the *International Journal of Nonprofit and Voluntary Sector Marketing*, printed ibid., p. 168.
28 ICM poll for the National Council of Voluntary Organisations, February 2005, op. cit.
29 Ibid.
30 Cathy Pharoah, 'Who Pays the Piper?', *Bond* magazine, www.bond.org.uk/networker/2002/sept02/paypiper.htm.
31 'When Two's a Crowd', research paper prepared by Dr Catherine Walker, CAF, 2002.

32 *Le Monde Diplomatique*, November 2004, accessed at www.globalpolicy.org/ngos/credib/2004/1104hinders.htm.
33 'Top 100 Firms Give Less Than 1% of Profits to Charity', Giving List 2004 special feature, *Society Guardian*, 8 November 2004.
34 'The Impact of the Tsunami Appeal on Charity Fundraising in the UK', Institute of Fundraising summary report, June 2005.
35 'Uncharitable Acts', Giving List 2004 special feature, *Society Guardian*, 8 November 2004.
36 ICM poll for the National Council of Voluntary Organisations, February 2005, op. cit.
37 Adapted from L. Salomon, S. Sokolowski and associates, *Global Civil Society: Dimensions of the Non-profit Sector*, vol. 2, Kumarian Press, 2004.
38 Figures for 2001, from Independent Sector, www.independentsector.org/programs/research/gv01main.html.
39 news.bbc.co.uk/1/hi/magazine/4075777.stm.
40 Beth Breeze, 'The Return of Philanthropy', Institute for Philanthropy, 2005; available at www.instituteforphilanthropy.org.uk.
41 Ibid.
42 *Global Civil Society: Dimensions of the Non-profit Sector*, op. cit.
43 L. Salomon, S. Sokolowski and List, *Global Civil Society: An Overview*, Johns Hopkins University Institute for Policy Studies, 2003, accessed at www.jhu.edu/~ccss/pubs/pdf/globalciv.pdf.
44 Ibid.
45 S. Devarajan, M.J. Miller and E.V. Swanson, *Goals for Development: History, Prospects and Costs, Volume 1*, World Bank, 2002, accessed at www.worldbank.org/html/extdr/mdgassessment.pdf.

46 For more information see 'Northern Ireland Charities: A Guide for Trustees' issued by the Department of Social Development Voluntary and Community Unit, www.dsdni.gov.uk/index/voluntary_and_community.htm.
47 The Statute of Charitable Uses Act (1601), 43 Elizabeth I c. 4, accessed at ksghome.harvard.edu/~phall/statute_of_charitable_uses.html.
48 *Income Tax Special Purpose Commissioners* v. *Pemsel* [1891] AC 531.
49 ICM Research poll for NCVO, accessed at www.icmresearch.co.uk/reviews/2003/ncvo-poll-feb-03.htm.
50 Annie Kelly and Emma Maier, *The Good Giving Guide*, Fusion Press (2004).
51 www.charityfacts.org.
52 www.amnesty.org.uk/amnesty/aiukstructure.shtml.
53 'Private Action, Public Benefit', Government Strategy Unit, 2002 – quoted in publication CC9, 'Campaigning and Political Activities by Charities', Charity Commission, September 2004.
54 Charity Commission guidance CC9, op. cit.
55 Interview with Melvin Coleman, finance director and company secretary of Amnesty International UK Section, 27 June 2005.
56 *The Size and Scope of the UK Voluntary Sector: NCVO Voluntary Sector Almanac 2004*, summary, available at www.ncvo-vol.org.uk.
57 Charities Aid Foundation website, www.cafonline.org.
58 'Hidden Homelessness: Britain's Invisible City', Crisis report, July 2004.
59 *The Good Giving Guide*, op. cit.
60 Pharaoh, 'Who Pays the Piper?', op. cit.

61 Tony Blair's speech to the NCVO annual conference 1999, available at www.ncvo-vol.org.uk/render.aspx?siteID=1&sID=18&subSID=206&documentID=1451.

62 Interview with the British Humanist Association, www.humanism.org.uk/site/cms/contentviewarticle.asp?article=1735&splash=yes.

63 D.T. Miller, J.G. Holmes and M.J. Lerner, 'Committing Altruism Under the Cloak of Self-interest: The Exchange Fiction', *Journal of Experimental Social Psychology*, vol. 38 (2002), summarised in *Stanford Business Magazine*, August 2003.

64 Alexis de Tocqueville, *Democracy in America*, 1835.

65 Charles Dickens, *Bleak House* (1853), chapter 15.

66 Oscar Wilde, 'The Soul of Man under Socialism', 1891.

67 Mary Wollstonecraft, *A Vindication of the Rights of Men*, 1790.

68 Quoted by Lord Philips of Sudbury in his address to the CAF annual conference, 11 November 2004.

69 Ian Ashbridge of Wrasse Records, interviewed in the *Guardian*, 2 June 2005.

70 Patrick West, *Conspicuous Compassion*, Civitas, 2004.

71 Interview with ABC Australia radio, accessed at www.abc.net.au/am/content/2004/s1051951.htm.

72 www.globalissues.org/TradeRelated/Debt/Scale.asp.

73 www.maketradefair.org.

74 'How Much Really Goes to Charity?', *Mirror*, 22 January 2005.

75 'Cancer Charity's Missing £11.5m', *Scotsman*, news.scotsman.com/topics.cfm?tid=865&id=582652003.

76 www.charityleaguetables.co.uk.

77 Conversation with Pesh Framjee, head of Deloitte Non Profit

Unit and Special Advisor to the Charity Finance Directors Group.
78 Conversation with Wendy Green, Charities Aid Foundation.
79 From www.charityfacts.org.
80 2003 Salary Survey, *Society Guardian*, 24 September 2003, society.guardian.co.uk/salarysurvey.
81 Charities Aid Foundation website, www.cafonline.org.
82 C. Walker, 'Altruism, Guilt and the Feel-good Factor: Why Do People Give to Charity?', *A Lot of Give*, op. cit., p. 147.
83 Keynote address by Prime Minister Tony Blair, NCVO Annual Conference, 1999.
84 Pharaoh, 'Who Pays the Piper?', op. cit.
85 Speech at London Metropolitan University, 29 May 2003, reprinted in the *Guardian*, society.guardian.co.uk/charityreform/story/0,11494,966616,00.html.
86 'How British Charity Was Silenced on Iraq', *Guardian*, 28 November 2003.
87 'Why Oxfam Is Failing Africa', *New Statesman*, 30 May 2005.
88 'Oxfam Bites Back', *New Statesman*, 6 June 2005.
89 Interview in the *Guardian*, 3 December 2003.
90 For the full analysis read David Rieff's excellent article at www.guardian.co.uk/arts/live8/story/0,16066,1513359,00.html.
91 'Zimbabwe Demands Reform to End Poverty', Action Aid press release, 25 April 2005, accessed at www.actionaid.org/index.asp?page_id=430.
92 Interview with Richard Miller, UK director of Action Aid, 27 June 2005.
93 E-mail interview with Kristyan Benedict, campaigns co-ordinator, Amnesty International UK, 21 July 2005.
94 Ibid.

95 'Bogus Tsunami Charities Lay Traps for British Volunteers', *The Times*, 12 April 2005, accessed at www.timesonline.co.uk/article/0,,2-1565777,00.html.
96 www.mercurynews.com/mld/mercurynews/new/11742273.htm, 26 May 2005.
97 Office of Fair Trading press release, January 2004, accessed at www.oft.gov.uk.
98 news.bbc.co.uk/cbbcnews/hi/newsid_4550000/newsid_4559500/4559585.stm.
99 www.national-lottery.co.uk/player/p/goodcauses/whereTheMoneyGoes.jsp.
100 news.bbc.co.uk/1/hi/uk_politics/2350455.stm.
101 news.bbc.co.uk/1/hi/uk/3601840.stm.
102 'Stopped: The £90k Beggars', *Mirror*, 25 August 2004.
103 'Doing Well and Doing Good', op. cit.
104 Interview with the author, 27 June 2005.
105 www.pfra.org.uk/facts_figures.htm.
106 'Chuggers: When Capitalism Works for Good', *New Statesman*, 11 October 2004.
107 'Public Irritation Forces Charities to End "Chugging"', *Observer*, 7 March 2004.
108 'Doing Well and Doing Good', op. cit.
109 The Giving Campaign Information for Donors, www.giving-campaign.org.uk/centrefr-4don.htm.
110 Suggestions from www.charityfacts.org.
111 *The Good Giving Guide*, op. cit., pp. 134–9.
112 Ibid.
113 Interview with Lindsay Boswell, CEO of the Institute of Fundraising, *Guardian*, 9 February 2005.
114 money.guardian.co.uk/smartspendingforchristmas/story/0,11127,1379159,00.html.

115 There are more case studies at www.bitc.org.uk/programmes/programme_directory/cause_related_marketing/casestudies.html.
116 Business in the Community Cause Related Marketing Tracker 2003, accessed at www.bitc.org.uk/resources/research/research_publications/crmtracker2003.html.
117 news.bbc.co.uk/1/hi/uk/2984069.stm.
118 *The Good Giving Guide*, op. cit., p. 54.
119 ICM Research survey commissioned by CSV Make A Difference Day and Barclays, 21 July 2004 (www.csv.org.uk/Campaigns/Make+a+Difference+Day/Research.htm).
120 TimeBank Employer Attitude Survey 2004, quoted in society.guardian.co.uk/volunteering/story/0,8150,1494096,00.html.
121 'Top 21 Unusual Volunteering Opportunities', TimeBank press release, 2 June 2005.
122 Charities Aid Foundation, www.cafonline.org.
123 legacies.cancerresearchuk.org/your_legacy/your_legacy_hub.asp.
124 Charities Aid Foundation/NCVO, *A Lot of Give*, op. cit.
125 Note: not all the agencies listed here participated in all the appeals in this section.
126 Executive Summary, Independent Evaluation of Expenditure of DEC Mozambique Floods Appeal Funds: March to December 2000. Independent evaluation conducted by Valid International and ANSA.
127 Executive Summary, Independent Evaluation: The DEC Response to the Earthquake in Gujarat January–October 2001. Independent evaluation conducted by Humanitarian Initiatives, UK, Disaster Mitigation Institute, Ahmedabad, and Mango, UK.

128 Executive Summary, Independent Evaluation of DEC Goma Crisis Appeal. Independent evaluation conducted by Carlo de Hennin and Patricia Kormoss.
129 Executive Summary, Independent Evaluation of the Disasters Emergency Committee's Southern Africa Crisis Appeal July 2002 to June 2003, Version 1.03 of 6 January 2003. Independent evaluation conducted by Valid International.
130 Executive Summary, Independent Evaluation of the Disasters Emergency Committee's Liberia Crisis Appeal August 2003–February 2004. Independent evaluation conducted by Peta Sandison.

Index

accounts, charities' 91–2
Action Aid 73, 101, 124, 129
administration costs 63–6
affinity credit cards 103
Africa Concern 124
agape 9
agricultural subsidies 62
All About Giving 136
Amnesty International 34, 46, 73–4
  donor numbers 82
  UK section (AIUK) 42, 43–4
  UK Section Charitable Trust 42
Ancient Order of Druids – Convalescent Home Fund 38
animal welfare 120
AOL Time Warner Foundation 136
'armchair action' 145
Armstrong, Lance 76
Association of Chief Executives of Voluntary Organisations (Acevo) 4, 65
asylum seekers 77–8

Baby Friendly Initiative 128
Band Aid 20 single 58
Beeton, Isabella 10–11
Benedict, Kristyan 73–4
Biafra 124
Big Issue Foundation 79
Blair, Tony 50, 68–9

blindness 127
Bono 57
Britain, comparison with other countries 25–8
British Heart Foundation (BHF) 116–17
British Red Cross 123, 129
BT 102
Bubb, Stephen 65
buildings, donation to charity 100
business, giving 24–5
Business in the Community (BITC) 25, 102
  Cause Related Marketing Tracker 102

Cadbury, George 12
Cadbury's 102–3
CAF *see* Charities Aid Foundation
CAFOD 100, 129
campaigning 48–9, 70–4
  guidance 42–3
cancer relief sector 106–7
Cancer Research Campaign 114
Cancer Research UK 107, 114–15
CARE International 129
Care, Rehabilitation and Aid for Sick Hedgehogs (CRASH) 37
Carnegie, Andrew 12–13
cause-related marketing 102
CCInet 136

Central Council of Church Bell
  Ringers Rescue Fund for
  Redundant Bells 39
charitable purposes 33–4, 44–5,
  148
  classification 33
charities
  accounts 91–2
  biggest international
    development 121–2
  biggest in UK 18, 113–14
  databases, listings and
    factsheets 137–40
  definition 147
  effectiveness 92–3
  information 135–7
  legitimacy checking 89–91
  numbers 14, 16–17, 41
  oldest in UK 11
  organisation types not
    qualifying 41
  registered 31–2
    advantages 40
    disadvantages 40–1
  registration number 89
  regulation 39–40
  sectors
    most popular 15–16, 109
    voluntary income by 110–11
  sources of income 19
  unusual 37–9
Charities Act 1993 91
Charities Aid Foundation (CAF)
  135–6, 147
  on charities' expenditure 66

Charity Account 88–9
  research 13, 19–20, 22
  websites 136
Charities Bill 43, 44–6, 81
Charities Direct 138
Charities Trust 141
Charity Bank 103
charity banking 103
Charity Check 141
Charity Choice 138
charity clothing collections,
  bogus 76
Charity Collections 141
Charity Commission 31, 33,
  39–40, 133–4, 148
  charities' accounts 91, 134
  guidance on political activity
    42–3
  role and powers 45, 133–4
  Safer Giving Code 93–5
  website 39, 133
Charity Facts 92, 139
'charity muggers' ('chuggers') 87,
  88, 148
Charity Portal 138–9
charity regulators 133–5
charity wristband 59, 76
CharityNet 136
Chaucer, Geoffrey 10
child protection 64, 119
child sponsorship 101–2, 127
Child Support Agency 8
ChildLine 102
children's rights 121
China 126, 128

Christian Aid 129
Christianity 9, 28
'chuggers' 87, 88, 148
Church of England 28
Citizens' Advice Bureaux (CABs) 63, 148
Citizenship Foundation 136
Civitas 60
Coffee Kids 102
Coleman, Melvin 81
community building 44, 68, 104
Community Service Volunteers (CSV) 144
complaints procedures 98
Concern Worldwide 124–5, 129
Corporate Community Investment 136
Councils for Voluntary Service (CVSs) 93, 147
Crisis 79

Darfur 2, 58
Data Protection Act 98
Dawkins, Richard 50
debt relief 62
Defaulting Charities list 39
Democratic Republic of Congo 131
Department for Social Development (Northern Ireland) 135, 148
Dickens, Charles 53–4
Disasters Emergency Committee (DEC) 2, 128–9
crises responded to 129–32

Do-it 105, 144
Donors' Charter 96–8, 140
Dunant, Henry 123

education, advancement 35
Egeland, Jan 66–7
Employee Volunteering 142
Etherington, Stuart 24
Ethiopia 72
Eton College 8, 34
Experience Corps 145

Federal Bureau of Investigation 74–5
feudal system 10
financial hardship relief 34–5
Food Commission 102
foundations, set up by businesses 24–5
'four heads' 33, 34–6
France 27
fundraising
by professional companies 94
costs 63–6
face-to-face 87–8
information 140–2

Gates, Bill 14
GDP 148
Geldof, Bob 59
Geneva Convention 123
Gift Aid 99, 149
gift lists 101
gift schemes 100–1
Gifts In Kind programme 125

GiveIt.co.uk 101
GiveNow 136
givers
  elite vs. others 80–2
  types 20
giving
  arguments against 53–82
    'absolving responsibility' 58–60
    'money not going where needed' 63–6
    'National Lottery enough' 77–8
    'patronising' 55–8
    'plugging gaps in society' 66–70
    'root causes not solved' 61–2
    'so many scams' 74–7
    'spare change to beggars' 78–80
    'too involved in politics' 70–4
    'undemocratic' 80–2
  by age group 19
  by sex 17–19
  by socio-economic class 19–21
  history 9–13
  levels recommended 28–9
  methods 87–9, 111–13
    new 21
    popularity and effectiveness 112–13
  overall 16–17
  protection 96–8
  questions to ask 86
  reasons for 47–52
  statistics 17–21
Giving Campaign 25, 28
Giving Nation programme 136
glossary of terms 147–9
goat, as gift 100
Goma Crisis Appeal 131
Goodgifts.org 100–1
Goodwill Gallery 138
government, role 22–3, 49, 69
GreatGifts.org 101
Greenpeace 88
gross domestic product (GDP) 148
GuideStar UK 90–1, 93, 137–8
Guidestar.org 90
Gujarat 130

Hall, Tony 65
Harkhuf 9
health charities, kind of donations 15
Help the Aged 129
Hillary, Sir William 117
homelessness charities 78–80
hospitals, private 34, 46

Imperial Cancer Research Fund 114
India 124, 130
India Earthquake Appeal 130
inheritance tax 106
Institute of Fundraising 96–8, 99, 140

international development/aid
charities 15, 64, 73, 109,
121–8
biggest 121–2
International Red Cross and Red
Crescent Movement 123
Iraq 70
Islam 9, 28
Islamic Relief 129
Israel 73–4
Italy 27

Japan 27
Jessop, Dr Augustus 58
Judaism 9–10, 28
Justgiving 141–2

Kenya 124
Korea 126

land, donation to charity
99–100
Langdon-Davies, John 126–7
legacy, definition 148
legacy giving 64, 106–7, 140
Li Ki 9
Liberia Crisis Appeal 132
Live Aid 72
Live8 concert 57, 59
Livestrong bracelets 76
Lost Musicals Charitable Trust
38

MacCollam, Reverend Joel 125
Macmillan, Douglas 118

Macmillan Cancer Relief 3,
118–19
Mactaggart, Fiona 71–2
Maimonides 9
Make Poverty History campaign
60, 71
Make Trade Fair campaign 71
market liberalisation 71
Médecins Sans Frontières (MSF) 2
membership schemes 98
Mengistu Haile Mariam 72
Merlin 129
Millennium Volunteers 146
Mozambique Floods Appeal
130
Muggeridge, Eric 126–7

National Association of Citizens'
Advice Bureaux 148
National Association of Councils
for Voluntary Service (NACVS)
147
National Council for Voluntary
Organisations (NCVO) 24, 70,
137, 148
consultation on charity sector 4
research 13, 20
Tony Blair conference address
50, 68–9
National Federation of
Community Organisations 93
National Lottery 77–8
National Society for the
Prevention of Cruelty to
Children (NSPCC) 64, 119

National Trust 98, 115
NCVO *see* National Council for Voluntary Organisations
Netherlands 27
New Philanthropy Capital (NPC) 139
NGO, definition 148
non-givers, reasons 21
non-profit sector, definition 149
Northern Ireland
  charitable status registration 32, 135
  Department for Social Development 135, 148
  Volunteer Development Agency 143
Norway 27
NSPCC 64, 119
Nurse, Sir Paul 8
Nyiragongo volcano 131

O'Brien, Ed 100
Office of Fair Trading 76
Office of the Scottish Charity Regulator (OSCR) 31–2, 40, 134–5, 148
Owen, Robert 12
Oxfam 34, 71, 100, 116, 129

Pakistan 124
Palestine 73–4
patronising 55–8
payroll giving 89, 100
Percol 102

philanthropy 9
  present-day 14
  Victorian 12–13, 53–5
'phishing' 75
pity 50–1
Plan International (UK) 126–7
political campaigning 48–9, 70–4
  guidance 42–3
poor relief, statutory system 10
poverty 61–2
private hospitals 34, 46
Professionals4free 144–5
protection donor 96–8
'public benefit' 33, 36–7, 45, 46, 81
  definition 149
Public Fundraising Regulatory Association (PFRA) 87–8, 140–1
public schools 46
purgatory 10
'purposes beneficial to community', examples 35–6

Radiohead 100
REACH 144
Red Cross 123, 129
Register of Charities 39, 133
regulation of charities 39–40
relationships, between giver and receiver 57–8
religion, advancement 35
Remember a Charity 140
Rieff, David 72

root causes, tackling 61–2
Roy, Arundhati 23
Royal National Lifeboat Institution (RNLI) 3, 23, 117
Royal Opera House 34, 65
Royal Society for the Protection of Birds 63
RSPCA 120

Safer Giving Code 93–5
salaries, charity workers' 63–6
Salvation Army 118
Sargeant, Professor Adrian 139
Save the Children UK 70, 120–1, 129
scams 74–7, 93–6
Schervish, Paul 14
Scotland, database of charities 135
Scottish Council for Voluntary Organisations (SCVO) 147
Shank, Bridget 75
shares, donation to charity 99
Shelter 79
Sight Savers International 127
smugness 58–60
social security 68
social services 48
social welfare 22
Society of Leather Technologists and Chemists Ltd 38
Southern Africa Crisis Appeal 131–2
sponsorship, of children 101–2, 127

sports clubs 46
spyware 75
Statute of Charitable Uses (1601) 10, 32–3
Stocking, Barbara 71
Student Volunteering England 146–7
Student Volunteering Week 147
Suzy Lamplugh Trust 101
Sweden 27

Tanzania 27
Tate, Henry 12
tax-efficient giving 98–100, 149
tax relief 99–100
Tearfund 129
Terrence Higgins Trust 64, 101
Thailand 75
TimeBank 105, 145
Tocqueville, Alexis de 51
tokenism 60
trade barriers 62, 71
Triodos Bank 103
trust 83
tsunami appeals 1–5, 75, 128–9
tzedakah 9–10, 28

UN 149
  Convention on the Rights of the Child 121
  foreign assistance guidelines 67
  Millennium Development Goals 28
UNICEF 128

UNICEF-UK 128
US
   giving 25–6
   self-interest motive 51
   tax incentives 26

'virtual volunteering' 145
Voluntary Agencies Directory 139
voluntary income 17
voluntary organisations, numbers 41
Voluntary Service Overseas (VSO) 146
volunteer, definition 149
Volunteer Centre Network Scotland 143
Volunteer Centres 144
Volunteer Development Agency (Northern Ireland) 143
Volunteer Development Scotland 143
volunteering 27, 96, 103–6
   benefits 105
   information 142–7
Volunteering England 105, 142
Volunteers' Week 145

Wales Council for Voluntary Action (WCVA) 142–3
websites, bogus 95–6
websites list
   www.actionaid.org 124
   www.allaboutgiving.org 136
   www.bhf.org.uk 116
   www.cafonline.org 135, 136

   www.cancerresearchuk.org 114
   www.ccinet.org 136
   www.charitiesdirect.com 138
   www.charitiestrust.org 141
   www.charity-commission.gov.uk 39, 133
   www.charitycheck.org.uk 141
   www.charitychoice.co.uk 138
   www.charitycollections.org 141
   www.charityfacts.org 92, 139
   www.charitynet.org 136
   www.charityportal.org.uk 138
   www.citizensadvice.org.uk 146
   www.citizenshipfoundation.org.uk 136
   www.communitymatters.org.uk 93
   www.concern.net 124
   www.csv.org.uk 144
   www.dec.org.uk 128
   www.do-it.org.uk 144
   www.dsdni.gov.uk 135
   www.employeevolunteering.org.uk 142
   www.experiencecorps.co.uk 145
   www.giveit.co.uk 101
   www.givenow.org 136
   www.goodgifts.org 100–1
   www.greatgifts.org 101
   www.guidestar.org.uk 137
   www.hedgehogs.org.uk 37
   www.howtogivetocharity.org 150
   www.institute-of-fundraising.org.uk 140

www.justgiving.com 141
www.macmillan.org.uk 118
www.millenniumvolunteers.
  gov.uk 146
www.nacvs.org.uk 147
www.nationaltrust.org.uk 115
www.ncvo-vol.org.uk 137
www.nspcc.org.uk 119
www.oscr.org.uk 134
www.oxfam.org.uk 116
www.pfra.org.uk 140
www.philanthropycapital.org
  139
www.plan-uk.org 126–7
www.professionals4free.org.uk
  144
www.redcross.org.uk 123
www.rememberacharity.org.uk
  140
www.rnli.org.uk 117
www.rspca.org.uk 120
www2.salvationarmy.org.uk 118
www.savethechildren.org.uk 120
www.scvo.org.uk 147
www.sightsavers.org.uk 127
www.studentvolunteering.org.
  uk 146
www.timebank.org.uk 145
www.unicef.org.uk 128
www.vds.org.uk 143
www.volunteering-ni.org 143
www.volunteering-wales.net
  143
www.volunteering.org.uk 142
www.volunteerscotland.info
  143
www.volunteersweek.org.uk 145
www.volwork.org.uk 144
www.vso.org.uk 146
www.wcva.org.uk 142
www.wer-uk.org 125
www.workwithus.org 143
www.worldvision.org.uk 126
Weddinglistgiving.com 101
Whelan, Robert 60
Wilde, Oscar 54–5
Wilson, Sir John 127
Woodland Trust 102
Wollstonecraft, Mary 57
World Emergency Relief (WER)
  125
World Food Programme 3
World Vision 101, 126
World Vision UK 126, 129
www. websites *see* websites list

Year of the Volunteer 104
Yell 102
Yellow Woods challenge 102
young people
  fundraising and giving 136
  volunteering 146–7

zakat 9, 28
Zimbabwe 73

50 Facts that Should Change the World

Jessica Williams

- A third of the world is at war

- Cars kill two people every minute

- America spends more on pornography than it does on foreign aid

- More than 150 countries use torture

Think you know what's going on in the world?

Jessica Williams will make you think again.

Read about hunger, poverty, human rights abuses, unimaginable wealth, the drugs trade, corruption, gun culture, the abuse of our environment and much more in this shocking bestseller.

'A research handbook for the *No Logo* generation' *Guardian*
'Fearless and compelling. You need to know what's in this book.' Monica Ali

Do Animals Have Rights?

Alison Hills

In December 1998, animal rights activist Barry Horne lay dying in prison on hunger strike. A convicted arsonist, he had decided to become a martyr to the cause. At the same time, the extremist Animal Rights Militia issued a hit list. If Horne died, ten 'vivisectionists' would be assassinated.

Animal rights is an emotive issue never far from the news. But it is often hard to know who to believe: radical animal rights protestors who claim that humans and animals should have equal rights; or scientists who argue that it is always legitimate to use animals for our benefit. Alison Hills examines the arguments for both sides and defends a practical ethics of animals which is both sensible and compelling.